S0-BGS-813

FAITH, STARS, AND STRIPES

the impact of Christianity on the
life history of America

A. Ronald Tonks and Charles W. Deweese

BROADMAN PRESS

Nashville, Tennessee

WITHDRAWN

13610

Pacific College - M. B. Seminary
Fresno, Calif. 93702

© Copyright 1976 • Broadman Press
All rights reserved
4265-22 (trade edition)
4288-04 (BRP)
ISBN: 0-8054-6522-7

Dewey Decimal Classification: 200.973
Subject Headings: U. S.—RELIGION // U. S.—CHURCH HISTORY
Library of Congress Catalog Card Number: 75-36888
Printed in the United States of America

**To
Ann Tonks and Mary Jane Deweese
Wives
who have offered
constant encouragement**

Preface

The relationship between American life in general and American religion in particular is a broad area. Nevertheless, one can't always take a nuts-and-bolts approach to American historical and religious studies if he expects to obtain a comprehensive view of the total picture. Individual trees are important, but the overarching themes which permeate an entire forest have their own merit. Selected themes—centering on the interpenetration of American religion and culture—are examined in the ten chapters which follow.

Many of the ideas presented here first took the form of five lectures delivered by the writers at Glorieta Baptist Conference Center on August 17-21, 1975, in the conference on "Southern Baptists and the Bicentennial," sponsored by the Christian Life Commission of the Southern Baptist Convention. Appreciation goes to the Christian Life Commission for providing this initial stimulus. Further refinement of the ideas in the book has come out of additional study and reflection. C. Welton Gaddy was especially helpful in reading Chapters 7-10 and in making suggestions for improvement.

The reader will notice that the names "United States" and "America" are used interchangeably in this writing. The writers are aware that America could be applied to any number of countries in North or South America. Without any attempt to deprive the name from other legitimate uses, America is used synonymously with the United States—following popular custom.

Permission is gratefully acknowledged for the use of the material in Chapter 4, which was first published as "Selected Highlights of the Baptist Heritage in America" in *Search*, Winter,

1976. © Copyright 1975, The Sunday School Board of the Southern Baptist Convention. All rights reserved.

Permission is also gratefully acknowledged for the use of the material in Chapter 7, which was first published as "Safeguarding the Right to Believe" in *Church Administration,* January, 1976.

© Copyright 1975, The Sunday School Board of the Southern Baptist Convention. All rights reserved.

A. RONALD TONKS & CHARLES W. DEWEESE

Contents

Introduction

The present writers owe more than a passing debt to Penrose St. Amant, currently president of the Ruschlikon Baptist Theological Seminary in Zurich, Switzerland. We are appreciative of the courses and seminars which he offered in American church history while a professor and dean of the School of Theology at the Southern Baptist Theological Seminary in Louisville, Kentucky.

St. Amant insisted on the necessity of studying American religion in the context of American culture, and on the impossibility of understanding American culture apart from the religious influences which helped to shape it. St. Amant's point seems obvious on the surface, but the tendency to separate religion and culture and to approach them as if they are mutually exclusive entities has resulted in a multitude of religio-cultural weaknesses.

One weakness has been the failure of many mainline Protestant denominations to view as a biblical mandate *the need to deal comprehensively with the social sicknesses in America.* A characteristic of large portions of American culture is a rugged form of individualism. Unfortunately, this individualism has often permeated Protestant expressions of Christianity to the degree that religion has become spiritualized and segregated from the corporate and multi-dimensional needs of suffering humanity.

Religion does have its private and individual features. Personal evangelism and the salvation of the individual are integral to the religious process. Soul competency, the priesthood of the believer, and the right of the individual to interpret the Bible for himself are basic concepts. But religion also has a bearing on the titanic social problems that confront America—abortion, aging, alcohol, capital punishment, crime, divorce, gambling, juvenile delinquency, pornography, poverty, race relations, sex, and war, just to name a few! (For religion to propel itself into the future in a spiritualized isolationism with minimal effort to confront the social threats to meaning in life and to life itself is a policy of evasion that is both non-biblical and impractical.)

Another weakness has been an erroneous interpretation of the American concept of the separation of church and state. Regretfully, this concept seems at times to be comprehended as even denying the legitimacy of communication between church and state. To the contrary, this cardinal precept in the First Amendment to the United States Constitution *allows and demands* interaction between church and state. It specifically prohibits the domination of the church by the state or the state by the church. It is inappropriate to claim that religion should have absolutely nothing to do with the state. This nonrelational mentality is the surest kind of rationalization by which American churches can escape potentially influential involvements in American politics. Such should not be the case. Religion ought to exert a powerful impact in the political arena.

C. Welton Gaddy recently wrote that the historic principle of church-state separation:

> . . . in no way prohibits the people of God from expressing their influence on or within government. Church and state are rightly separated for the good of both, but Christianity and governmental concerns can never be separated except at the expense of both.[1]

Gaddy also pointed out that the cliche, "Christianity and politics don't mix," with its assumption that politics is inherently evil, has resulted in a widespread failure to encourage young people desiring political careers. "Politics as a viable form of Christian ministry has received little support." [2] Thus, the church cannot detach itself from the state and its political aspects to the extent that prophetic judgments become powerless, and the two realities proceed into eternity like parallel lines which never meet.

A third weakness has been the reluctance of American culture to give proper acknowledgement to the religious forces which have helped mold it. Two examples from Baptist life will show that such forces have been strong. (At several places in this book, illustrations will be employed which are derived out of Baptist life. The points being made will usually have application to a broader scope of religious life in America.)

The first example relates to cultural life on the early American frontier, including such places as Kentucky and Tennessee from about 1780 to 1840. Churches had a decided effect on the moral climate of the untamed frontier. To be sure, "early Baptist churches were in a very real sense moral courts. In all cases they supplemented, and in many cases superseded, the civil courts of the land." [3]

The churches earned the reputation of being moral courts through the rigorous use of discipline. This discipline "served as a practical corrective aid to some of the excesses of frontier life." [4] Because of generally lawless conditions, the frontier stood in need of restraint. In comparison to their number, the churches exerted a disproportionate influence on frontier communities. The churches, Baptist and others, "were an important—if not the most important—factor in maintaining decency and order in the average frontier community." [5]

The second example relates to Baptist education and American culture. Owning sixty-seven senior colleges and universities in America in 1974,[6] Baptists have contributed significantly to the educational improvement of American culture. Baptists have helped to shape the moral climate of America through their stress on theological education and the effective ministries which result from it. Baptist support of female education (by 1900 there were no less than twenty-three Baptist colleges for women in the South) [7] has helped elevate the status of women in American society. Further, Baptists exerted a major influence on the use of public schools in America. The 600 Baptist academies and schools which arose in the South between 1800 and 1920 [8] often preceded and encouraged the growth of public schools. Last, millions of Americans have profited from the perennial Baptist opposition to sectarianism in public schools.

The interdenominational Sunday school movement has also made a strong impression on culture in America. Through training in Bible knowledge and the development of conscientious Christian citizens, the movement has aided the moral climate in America. The movement has stimulated reforms in American life. It even originated to train poor children who had no other chance for education. Also, the movement helped sponsor the development of public, free education. After dropping secular subjects from their curriculum in order to offer only religious education, Sunday schools became hearty advocates of public, free schools where children could become knowledgeable in secular subjects.

A fourth religio-cultural weakness has been the failure of American religion to see the rapid speed with which it accommodates itself to the culture. Standards for entrance into church membership are frequently relaxed and easy. Church attendance is in constant combat with television, increased mobility, and recreational outlets. Suburban religion has a rather easygoing God, a tendency to identify middle-class values with Christian values, and an inadequate sensitivity to the power of social structures.

Evidence of the moral decline in America is clear when a leading non-theological news magazine asks, "What's Happening to American Morality?" [9] The presence of violence on television, of pornography on the bookstands, 40,000,000 handguns in American hands, and corruption in government—among other things—point up "a tidal wave of changing standards that is creating widespread moral bewilderment, concern and resentment." [10]

American religion has not escaped these trends. Religion is

involved in culture and conditioned by it. American religion must confront a basic question: to what extent will it allow culture to define and influence the nature of its existence? A complementary question follows: does American religion possess the resources, the discipline, and the desire to ward off the forces of secularism which are invading it with the relentlessness of an air hammer?

The last religio-cultural weakness to be mentioned is the failure of American churches to discern the strength of the moral impact they are capable of producing on the culture in which they exist. Apart from American religion, American culture would probably be totally depraved and degenerate. The fact is, however, that religion has put much moral fiber and substance into culture. The presence of God, the Bible, buildings for worship and study, and committed followers of God are not superficial accoutrements on the American scene. They are integral to America and have made an enormous impact on cultural life.

Still, there are minorities living in wretched conditions, families that are disintegrating, alcohol and drug problems that are achieving epidemic proportions, outbreaks of violence that are becoming increasingly widespread, breakdowns in integrity that are becoming far too pervasive, and numerous other problems. The churches of America are fully capable of helping to solve these ailments on a more intensive basis than at present. Will the churches acquiesce to the mounting tumults or will they seek and implement creative solutions?

Duke K. McCall recently illustrated rather concretely how it is possible for the moral forces of American religion to be called out of reserve and applied to the problem of "moral garbage" television is pumping into millions of homes. "It is time," he claimed, "to focus what moral indignation the Christian church can generate on the prime force of moral pollution," [11] namely, television.

Thus, McCall suggested two steps. First, hit at the "sensitive nerve of the television industry" by writing the sponsor or sponsors of a program advising them that you will not purchase their product because of its association with something you interpret as immoral. Second, write the Federal Communications Commission, 1919 M Street, Washington, D.C. 20554, and send a copy of this letter to your senator or congressman. McCall concluded:

> I know that I am advocating tough tactics. But if you do not mind the moral erosion of America, do not complain when you are robbed or raped. The odds that both will happen to your family are rising—thanks, in part, to ABC, NBC, and CBS.[12]

The preceding five weaknesses in the relationship between religion and culture in America gave some of the impetus to the writing of this book. The purposes of the writers are: (1) to demonstrate that faith in God has been an essential ingredient in conditioning both the ideals and the practice of American life from the beginning, (2) to depict some of the patterns of interpenetration which have and do occur between religion and culture in America, and (3) to propose modifications which the Christian perspective seems to suggest, both for the American concept of freedom and "The American Dream." The role of Christianity will assume a prominent position in this work.

Justification for the breadth of this subject resides in the need for all Americans to be acquainted with some of the general religious themes which have affected their national heritage. If culture is the "constellation" of values by which a community defines the meaning of its existence,[13] then the only way to understand a community or nation in the past or present is to know what its values are—social, political, religious, and others. It is also helpful to know the degrees of importance attached to various kinds of values. The contention of these writers is that religious values, however submerged they may appear to be in the present, have been some of the most powerful determining forces in the nation's history. Further, in the face of considerable resistance, these forces have the potential to rise up and stimulate a resurgence of moral integrity and justice. It cannot be denied that "religion has been a major force in the shaping of America and that the religious dimension must continue to be taken with the utmost seriousness if 'liberty and justice for all' are to have a solid foundation." [14]

The religious expression which predominates in this writing is Christian in thrust. This is not to suggest that the United States is a Christian nation, but to assert the objective belief that Christianity has exerted a more formative impact on American development than any other religious expression. Neither is this to deny that Judaism and other religious forms have transformed American culture in a variety of positive ways. They obviously have, and commendation is in order.

Hopefully, this writing will achieve five basic results. The first will be a few fresh insights into the religious identity of America. No one set of concepts can adequately convey the qualities, reason for being, and goals of a nation. Economic, military, political, social, psychological, geographical, religious, and other concepts and interpretations have to be properly balanced to arrive at a true national picture. An economic interpretation cannot explain the appeal for liberty and justice. A military view in no way explains the call for equality and fraternity. A political explanation cannot account for the unalienable rights deemed appropriate for all men. A social description of American history is unable to justify the words "In God We Trust," which appear so prevalently on coins and currency. A psychological definition cannot understand the invisible, yet powerful, factors which underlie the sacrificial life-style of a person like Luther Rice. A geographical depiction is at a loss in pointing to the Christian commitment of millions of American citizens.

Religion must be placed in proper perspective among all the other elements that explain a nation. The essential insight conveyed in this book, however, is that the role of religion goes much further in explaining America than has often been credited. Because of their personal involvement as religionists in America, the writers do not wish to claim a greater historical influence for religion than it deserves. They do wish to state unapologe-tically that religion has played a major role in the growth of the United States, and that the potential of its moral and spiritual influence has never been tapped.

The second desired result of this writing will be additional study into the religious history of America by the readers. It is surprising to discover how little knowledge most Christians have concerning the history of their own denomination and church life. Every Christian should familiarize himself with both the immediate and the more general historical context from which he has sprung.

To illustrate a logical approach for study, a Baptist who is a member of the First Baptist Church of Nashville, Tennessee, would do well to read a history of that church, a history of the Nashville Baptist Association to which the church belongs, a history of the Tennessee Baptist Convention in which the church has membership, a history of the Southern Baptist Convention, as well as a book dealing generally with the religious history of America.

To insure that the preceding religious histories are understood in their political, economic, and social context, it would be advisable to read as complementary material a general history of Nashville, one of Davidson County, one of Tennessee, and one of the United States. This complementary reading is impera-tive. How, for example, can one understand the religious history of the South without some insight into the wider social and economic discussion of cotton and slavery?

Ideally, the third result of this work will be an increase in the critical loyalty which each reader has for the United States and for his own church and denomination. The reader can take one of four stances in reference to his country, and his church and denomination.[15] (1) He can be critical and not loyal. This means he is perceptive in identifying problem areas but non-constructive in finding and implementing solutions. (2) He can be loyal and not critical. This means that his commitment is blind and superficial. (3) He can be neither critical nor loyal. This implies that there is no dedication at all. (4) He can be both critical and loyal. This indicates that his commitment is genuine, but he is unwilling to settle for an unquestioning attitude when moral compromise is at stake. This person has no room for the "love America or leave it" mentality. Rather, he knows that love and respect demand occasional discipline and rebuke, and that it is only through the cultivation of loyalty that he even earns the right to be critical.

The fourth result desired from this writing is renewed obedience to God on the part of the nation and the individuals comprising it. References to God on coins and currency, in the pledge of allegiance and other national documents, in courtroom settings, and other prominent places are prevalent. Consistency between alleged faith and responsible action creates two options for Americans. Either they can eliminate the references to God from these places and abandon him, or they can take seriously the commitment to God which was inherent in the formation of this country. Selection of the former option will run counter to the traditional American understanding that this country is in some sense related to God. Selection of the latter will add substance to American commitment to God. If America believes that it is so important to include references to God in prominent places, then this achievement of consonance between faith and practice demands a new allegiance to God.

The fifth result expected from this writing is a resurgence of interest in applying religious and moral principles, based on obedience to God, to the totality of American life. The accomplishment of this must obviously be prefaced by an awareness of the characteristics of American culture and civilization. Penrose St. Amant mentioned several such characteristics.[16]

(1) *Optimism*—The United States is still an adolescent compared to the age of most European countries. In her youth, America is grounded in a vision of unlimited hope. The idea prevails that Americans can do just about anything they want to do if they have enough time, consultations, and studies.

(2) *Willingness to experiment*—This goes back to Puritanism and to the frontier struggles for survival. An innovative spirit stimulates Americans to launch into the unknown and either make new discoveries or break old records. New creations are sometimes of limited duration, especially when they turn out to be mere fads.

(3) *A practical or pragmatic temper*—Americans tend to be a non-ideological people who accept the dictum of John Dewey and William James that something is good if it works. The usefulness, workability, and functional capacity of a new invention are considered paramount. Aesthetic and ideological values are frequently given second-rate status in the scheme of priorities.

(4) *A certain distrust of the intellectual and of intellectual matters*—This can be traced, in part, to the American frontiersmen who considered survival more important than education. Even in the educational enterprise, there is a certain mistrust of the intellectual who is responsibly critical of the things about him. This distrust fails to recognize that criticism is in the very nature of education, and that it makes the difference between education and propaganda.

(5) *Technology*—This is applied science. It expresses itself in skyscrapers, bridges, jets, automation, and other things. Technological achievements are diverse: American spacecraft capable of linking up with those of other nations in a spirit of cooperation and peaceful co-existence, but also nuclear arsenal capable of destroying most human life on the planet earth. National values will ultimately determine whether technology is used for good or ill.

(6) *Urbanization*—Cities are increasing in size (geographically and by population) and in number. The urban revolution tends to create conformity and depersonalization. These traits produce negative results when millions of people find themselves lonely and without friends. The traits are not entirely negative, however, for a certain sense of liberation can often come through anonymity.

(7) *Enormous power*—The United States has enormous military

strength with a large percentage of its annual budget going for defense purposes. The country possesses political prestige around the world as reflected in continuous international negotiations. The country has a monopoly on many of the world's resources and is able to exert power in trade agreements. In comparison to her size and age, the United States is obviously a strong country—although she is gradually and certainly having to come to terms with the powers of other nations.

(8) *A certain vitality*—This is related to the youth of the nation. Things do not move along at a static pace saturated with unyielding trends. There is a virility to the American way which sometimes ends in substantive achievements and at other times manifests itself in a sterile activism.

(9) *Great affluence*—The United States and its citizens are rich compared to most countries and citizens of those countries. Nevertheless, there are significant pockets of poverty in America. One of the real ironies of the American way resides precisely in this contrast between the increasing wealth of some and the increasing poverty of others.

Only after religious forces begin to comprehend the preceding characteristics of American life, plus others, can these forces make a solid impact on the nation. In some instances, these forces can influence the American dream only by accommodating themselves to certain points of American distinctiveness. For example, the technological side of American life can be penetrated by religious principles only as religion makes full advantage of technology (such as televised worship services) for its own purposes. Monastic retreat from technology would result in the failure of religion to compete with all the other modern forces vying for a position of importance in American society.

Readers can use this book helpfully in one of two ways, apart from the individual reading of it. *First, a study group can be formed inside or outside the church.* This group can use the broad concepts conveyed in the book as a launching pad for more detailed study of selected subjects. Questions which can be raised and discussed include the following: (1) What were some of the religious influences on the founding fathers of the United States? (2) What impact did religious concepts make on the development of important early American documents? (3) What role did religion play in the rise of early American culture? (4) Has the Christianization of America ever been achieved? (5) To what degree has the basic thrust of American religion been modified by American culture? (6) Are there facets of religion in America which have accommodated themselves so completely to American culture that they are no longer able to maintain an ethical or prophetic tension with the culture? (7) What is the present status of freedom in America? (8) What are some principles and guidelines by which American citizens and churchmen can deal creatively with the freedom struggle? (9) What are some of the key elements in the American dream? (10) Are there themes within the Christian hope by which the American dream might profit?

Second, an organization can sponsor an essay contest based on some of the themes suggested in this book. Each essayist would use supplementary materials in order to get a more complete picture of the particular theme about which he or she writes. Three categories could be established and three awards given. One category could relate to historical treatments of specific phases of the interaction between religion and culture in America. The second category could consist of analyses of individual facets of contemporary interrelationships between religion and culture. The third category could be comprised of responsible, but speculative, looks into the future co-existence of religion and culture.

Possible topics which could be explored in such an essay are:

John Hart: Baptist Signer of the Declaration of Independence
Religious Influences Behind the First Amendment
The Role of Religion in Taming the American Frontier
American a Christian Nation: Pros and Cons

Present Status of the Separation of Church and State
Freedom Concerns of Highest Importance to Americans
Indications of the Acculturation of American Religion
The Prospects for Religion in American Life
Requirements for the Preservation of Religious Liberty
Features of the Christian Hope
Aspects of the American Dream
The Christian Hope and the American Dream in Creative
   Tension.

1.
Religious Life of
Early American Leaders

Although many of the specific historical facts about the beginnings of the United States of America are known, perhaps nothing is more shrouded in mystery and myth than these beginnings. The date, July 4, 1776, stands out as the formal birth of the republic, although July 2, 1776, was the day twelve colonies (New York did not vote) decided officially to separate from Britain. In reality, the beginning of the United States can be traced back hundreds of years to the struggles for freedom and the acceptance of the rule of law in the British Isles.

Who are the founders of America? Should such names as Cotton Mather, William Bradford, Roger Williams, and others from the seventeenth century be included? Do Peter Stuyvesant, William Penn, and other governors in the late seventeenth and early eighteenth centuries deserve a place of honor? Should one include Jonathan Edwards, Theodore Frelinghuysen, George Whitefield, and other religionists on the list?

The common and unsophisticated people should also be considered as founders, for had it not been for their acceptance of the American way of life, all leadership would have faltered. One is reminded of the statement attributed to the late King George VI of the United Kingdom. The king, as his custom was, visited a group of his citizens who had just suffered severe bomb damage during World War II. One man said, with great feeling, "You are a great king, sir." With tears in his eyes, the king answered simply, "You are a great people."

Certainly in the strictly literal sense, the founders of America were those who not only supported the American Revolution but, at the same time, had a concrete part in molding American freedom and independence. But for practical purposes the list must be selective and include only the principal founders.

Each nation has produced leaders to assist in a time of special need, and the United States of America is no exception. The success of the American Revolution and the growth of America into a large super-power with a population in excess of two hundred million have assured the founders of this country a prominent place in the English-speaking world, if not the entire world.

Elbert Thomas, a United States Senator from Utah, in his book, *This Nation Under God,* suggests that probably in no other period of recorded history was there a "larger number of human figures touched by eternal greatness" than during the time of the American Revolution and early rational period.[1] In spite of such statements, which have been amplified by history, it is true that this period abounded with great men. While some would suggest that this was evidence of God's divine providence, it is certainly fair to assert that such a situation was the result of a people infiltrated with religious faith and reliance upon God; in other words, not miracles, but religious strength. When Ethan Allen and his Green Mountain boys attacked Fort Ticonderoga and demanded its surrender, they were asked in whose name such a demand was being made. Allen replied, "In the name of the Great Jehovah and the Continental Congress."

Certainly, the whole is the sum of all its parts. While the foundations of the United States of America were being laid, most of the people were hardly aware of it. The distinctive characteristics of the American people had ripened and were spreading throughout the colonies long before the revolution. It is dangerous, and to a degree erroneous, to interpret America solely on the basis of its leaders; and yet, were it not for the leaders, it would be impossible to have a country. In a sense, the leaders shaped the destiny of America and built the initial superstructure upon the foundation made by the people.

There was a sense of equality among the people in early America. Except for the slave population, the poor were less poor than in Europe, and the rich were not as wealthy. The distribution of wealth in colonial America was far more equal than in Europe.[2] There were certainly differences of social position in early America, but as R. R. Palmer put it, "Rank somehow lacked the magic it enjoyed in Europe."[3]

In the emigrations from Europe to America, the comfortably wealthy and high-born were noticeably absent. In one sense, the American Revolution became an attempt to preserve a society that already existed. It is also true that in the Revolution, the United States permanently lost an important nucleus of conservatism. In fact, until most recent times, the Loyalists have been overlooked and, for the most part, made invisible. "The 'American consensus' rests in some degree on the elimination from the national consciousness, as well as from the country, of a once important and relatively numerous element of dissent."[4]

Certainly, as we attempt to examine the religious persuasions of a select group of the founding fathers, we must ask what about religion in general in Revolutionary America? The role played by religion in the American Revolution is widely disputed. It has become popular, at times, to stress the great religious principles of the founders of the United States. Writing in 1786, John Adams, referring to the founding leaders of America, said: "It will never be pretended [that these men] had interviews with the gods, or were in any degree under the inspiration of Heaven, more than those at work on ships or houses, or laboring in merchandise or agriculture; it will forever be acknowledged that these governments were contrived by reason and the senses."[5]

An aggressive anti-Christianity never developed in America. Its failure to develop was not rooted in the fact that the American revolutionary leaders were warmly religious, but rather because no religious body seriously opposed the revolutionary position.[6] It is true, however, that the Anglican clergy generally opposed the revolution, mainly because of that church's close connection with British authority. Such opposition did not pose a serious threat in most instances, since those clergymen were in general easily removed from their pulpits.

Most Americans both before and during the Revolution did not belong to any church. Palmer has stated that a constant moving of the country's population was responsible for such a situation.[7] Most of the founding fathers were strongly in favor of the most enviable human virtues, but in most instances, they saw no connection between these virtues and religious practice. They were generally deists and were perhaps best typified by Benjamin Franklin who, at age twenty-two, wrote his *Articles of Belief and Acts of Religion.* Franklin accepted the existence of a Supreme Being and listed some spiritual values including "his hope he would 'refrain from censure, calumny, and detraction; that I may avoid and abhor deceit and envy, fraud, flattery, and hatred, malice, lying, and ingratitude.' "[8] He also wished to " 'possess integrity and evenness of mind, resolution in difficulties, and fortitude under affliction . . . tenderness for the weak and reverent respect for the ancient . . . kind[ness] to my neighbors, good-natured to my companions, and hospitable to strangers.' "[9] These are admirable qualities but hardly more than a bland humanism, and certainly not a Christ-centered belief.

There are seven "fathers of America" to note especially, not because they are typical or atypical of the religious beliefs of all, but rather because each in his own way played a most significant role in the young republic. The list is comprised of Benjamin Franklin, George Washington, Thomas Jefferson, James Madison, Alexander Hamilton, John Jay, and John Dickinson. Some may say, "Why not John Adams, Patrick Henry, Thomas Paine, Richard Lee, or even John Hancock?" But it is those who debated and framed the governmental instruments upon which the United States has been built that should be considered first.

Benjamin Franklin was born in Boston in 1706, the fifteenth child of a candle maker. He was christened at Old South Church and dedicated to the Christian ministry. Limited finances prevented his receiving an education, so he learned the printer's trade. The rigid Puritanism of Boston soon prompted him to run away to Philadelphia. At the time of this move, he made a remarkable resolution to turn from his boisterous way of life to one more noted for good manners and avoidance of controversy.

Franklin's lack of formal education prompted him to seek continuously to learn, but knowledge by itself was meaningless to him unless it was tied to a proper attitude toward people and life in general. "I have always thought that one man of tolerable abilities may work great changes and accomplish great affairs among mankind, if he first forms a good plan and . . . makes execution of that same plan for his sole study and business." [10] Franklin expressed a self-confident humanism divorced from both established religion and Christ-centered theology. Yet during the heat of debate and controversy at the Philadelphia Constitutional Convention, when it looked like the Convention would dissolve into disunity, Franklin could declare: "The longer I live, the more convincing proofs I see of this truth—that God governs in the affairs of men. And if a sparrow cannot fall to the ground without his notice, is it probable that an empire can rise without his aid?" [11]

The paradox of Franklin's religious belief is seen also in his desire at the same meeting to be certain that each session convened with prayer. Here Franklin asserted his dependence upon a higher power but also his desire to secure a commitment among men to attempt their best in a troubled time. In a certain sense, at Philadelphia, he succeeded; yet this expression of positive religious faith may be linked to the pragmatic Franklin who, when writing to Benjamin Vaughan on November 9, 1779, ostensibly to prove the doctrine of fate, said, "As prayer can produce no change in things that are ordained, praying must then be useless and an absurdity." [12]

The religious beliefs of Franklin cannot be explained in simple terms. Among other things, he was a sermon-taster and preferred listening to those sermons of George Whitefield that had been preached elsewhere because he felt Whitefield improved with each delivery. The excellence of presentation seemed to be more important to Franklin than the content.

Franklin fluctuated in his religious beliefs. He accepted the moral system of Jesus but rejected the Messiah and Christ of the Scriptures.

George Washington was born in Virginia (1732) to a socially important Episcopal family. When he was eleven, his father died, and his half-brother, Lawrence, a devout churchman, became his guardian. Washington received only five years of formal schooling. At age fifteen, he became a surveyor and travelled extensively. Particularly during his travels on the frontier, Washington met dissenters who had gone there to escape religious oppression. Many of them came to respect this young man who acquired a reputation for fairness in his dealings with people and had a genuine interest in individuals. Largely because of these factors, he was elected to the Virginia House of Burgesses at age twenty-four and later served in the state militia, rising finally to be the commander of the Continental Army.

Washington was a conciliator, and perhaps as much as anyone in the early republic, one who made the new government work. In fact, there is little doubt that he was the main force which held the new country together. It was he who in 1775 ordered members of the army to "discontinue profane cursing, swearing and drunkenness." [13] This theme was repeated throughout the orders he gave during the dark days of 1778. To him patriotism included loyalty to God, as well as political matters. He stated, "We can have little hopes of the blessing of Heaven on our Arms, if we insult it by our impiety and folly." [14]

Because of his compromising spirit, Washington was able, as the political leader, to hold the various factions together. In fact, he was the only man who had the universal support of the convention. When he became president, he continued his tolerant practices, and at times it becomes difficult to determine his true religious beliefs. As it is with so many political leaders, it would be easy to take portions of his writings and draw different conclusions.

Washington was an Episcopalian, although after he became

president, he never partook of communion. His reasons were probably more political than religious. He did not want the newly-formed country to become wedded to one particular Christian group. He also had a strong sense of privacy, and this is one area he did not want exploited. Whatever his personal beliefs were, he was certainly not an atheist as some have suggested. He was likely a deist with a strong overlay of frontier dissent. Writing in 1793, Washington said, "In this Land of equal liberty it is our boast, that a man's religious tenets will not forfeit the protection of the Laws, nor deprive him of the right of attaining and holding the highest offices that are known in the United States." [15]

Thomas Jefferson, like Washington, was raised in a devout Episcopal family. Much of his training was done by ministers. He was a man of innumerable talents and creatively used his broad education and knowledge gained from reading widely concerning the major issues of his day.

When Jefferson grew older, he listed three accomplishments of which he was most proud for his epitaph: (1) author of the Declaration of Independence, (2) author of the Statute of Virginia for religious freedom, and (3) father of the University of Virginia. Jefferson became highly involved in the cause for religious liberty in Virginia. He suggested that that particular struggle was the bitterest fight of his life.

Although Jefferson has frequently been accused of holding no religious beliefs at all, nothing could be further from the truth. His insistence on individual rights—which permitted a person to follow his beliefs—was mistakenly interpreted as an attack on all denominational religion. Although author of the Virginia bill establishing religious freedom, he remained generally aloof from any specific denominational grouping. Like Washington, he did not want any debate over his personal religious views while he was in the service of his country.

After his retirement, he wrote frequently and specifically about religious matters. He prepared what he considered to be his "Bible," *The Life and Morals of Jesus,* a collection of what he believed about the morals and teachings of Jesus. Writing to his friend, Benjamin Rush, Jefferson said that his religious beliefs were the result of a lifetime of reflection and were quite different from the anti-Christian beliefs of which he was accused. "To the corruptions of Christianity I am indeed opposed, but not to the genuine precepts of Jesus himself." [16] He went further to assert that his belief in Jesus was bound to his human accomplishments—a very low Christology and one most evangelicals would assert was something less than the full knowledge of Christ, the divine-human Lord of the New Testament.

James Madison ought to be included in this list of founding fathers because he above any other person assisted in making the Constitution workable and practical. Madison is remembered for his part in the Constitutional Convention and as president of the United States, but he also worked vigorously on behalf of religious liberty. He secured the acceptance in Virginia of Jefferson's statute on religious freedom, and—vigorously assisted by John Leland, a Virginia Baptist minister—the passage of the Bill of Rights (the first ten amendments to the Constitution of the United States).

Madison was well-trained theologically and had studied for the ministry. Then, later in his life, he continued his religious studies systematically. Despite his wide knowledge, he referred only rarely to his personal religious beliefs. He was apparently a deist and later a Unitarian. Clearly in his day he was champion of the persecuted minority. The story of Madison and the Baptists has been related many times. In fact, without their combined influence, the story of religious liberty in America and throughout the world would be vastly different.

The consuming passion of Madison's religious life was religious freedom. He affirmed: "Freedom to believe in a creed or religion or freedom not to believe must be a basic right in any democratic society." [17]

Alexander Hamilton is one of the most intriguing of the founders. He was born on the island of Nevis in the British West Indies in 1755 or 1757. He began to work between the ages of eleven and thirteen as clerk for a trading firm in St. Croix. In 1772 he came to the American colonies to study and enrolled in King's College, New York.

After 1776 he rose quickly to aide-de-camp to George Washington. At the Philadelphia Constitutional Convention he made the major contribution of his life—the formulation of the federal system of government. He has been considered an aristocrat by many, and yet he was raised on the ideas of John Locke and David Hume.

In his early life, he seems to have given religion only passing thought, although he wrote a short statement that seems to suggest a modified deism. The supreme being created man, but at the same time endowed man with the right to personal liberty and personal safety. Hamilton never affiliated with any religious group, but in the eighteenth century this would not have indicated a lack of piety.

There are four phases in Hamilton's religious life. As a young man, he was devout and religious in the traditional Christian sense, receiving support and encouragement from some Presbyterian clergymen for his education. He had warm friends in both the Presbyterian and Episcopal churches but never decided to join either.

The second stage in his religious life was one of indifference—from 1777 to 1792 when his published writings contained only limited references to God. Several stories persist that Hamilton made some wisecracks about God at the Constitutional Convention of 1787. He is reported to have quipped on the Convention floor, when Franklin moved that future sessions be opened with prayer, that there was no need for "foreign aid." [18] Despite his marriage to the devout Betty Schuyler, who was nicknamed "the saint," Hamilton never joined her church, which was the Reformed Church.

The third stage is best described as an acceptance of a quasi-religious or opportunistic belief. He wedded the country he loved with the Christian God he thought he knew. He used religious slogans to buttress the Federalist Party's power. He wanted to mobilize the religious forces of America to accomplish his human ends. "Actually it is during these years when religious slogans were so often on his lips that Hamilton seems farther from God and from any understanding of his Son, Jesus Christ, than at any time in his whole career." [19]

The final stage occurred following the frightful night in which he was mortally wounded in a duel with Aaron Burr. On his death bed, Hamilton called for a clergyman to administer the Lord's Supper. Bishop Moore of the Episcopal church at first refused because of the opposition of his church to dueling. The Presbyterian clergyman, Dr. John Mason, refused because his church forbade the administration of the Lord's Supper in private. Moore returned a day later, and, convinced of Hamilton's piety and desire to denounce dueling, administered the Lord's Supper. The following day, Hamilton died.

The question remains. What prompted this change of heart from cynicism to devotion? There may be several factors which differ little from those of modern man. Hamilton was frustrated as he fell rapidly from political power between 1799 and 1800. In fact, he experienced one of the most rapid demises from power of any political leader in America, apart perhaps from that of Richard Nixon. In 1801, Hamilton's oldest son, Philip, was killed in a duel, and his oldest daughter, so over-wrought by his death, became insane. It is probably fair to say that Hamilton, like so many, knew the Christian faith but waited almost too long to accept it.

John Jay, a New Yorker, was from one of the most prominent families of that area. Jay was a conservative in many respects including religion. It surprised many Loyalists that such a prominent high-born person would support the American Revolution. He rose from Chief Justice of New York to President of the Revolutionary Continental Congress. He then became roving foreign ambassador, founded the Federalist party, was the first Chief Justice of the United States, ambassador to Britain and the negotiator of Jay's treaty, and finally became governor of New York.

Jay was perhaps the most traditional in religion of all the founding fathers. When it was proposed that the sessions of the First Continental Congress be opened with prayer, Jay opposed such a move. He contended there was too much religious diversity among the members for the prayers to be effective. His religious views were in sharp contrast to those of Jefferson, Franklin, or John Adams. Jay attended church regularly and opposed deistic views. He was one of the early presidents of the American Bible Society, of which his son, William, was the founder. In his years at Bedford, New York, he attended the Presbyterian church, but he still continued to support Episcopal views.

John Dickinson is also a significant founding father of the United States. Although he attended the Second Continental Congress and assisted in the preparation of some of the documents, he refused to sign the Declaration of Independence, because he felt such a move was premature. Later he was largely responsible for formulating the Articles of Confederation, which in turn led to the Philadelphia Constitutional Convention.

Dickinson did not widely circulate his religious views. Although he died a Quaker, he appears to have nominally accepted a modified deism. Dickinson makes mention of God but apparently as though he did not know him intimately.

The founding fathers' religion: myth and reality? Most acknowledged a divine being. Some, such as Washington and Jefferson, were reluctant to publicize their specific beliefs because of their official governmental positions. Others, such as Hamilton, searched for a more perfect faith, but in the end few of them apparently achieved it. By and large, religion was used politically then, as much as today. The founding fathers as a group were atypical of most other groups in America. In other words, they accepted divine faith in a similar ratio to that of most other groups. There was, as in most leadership groups, a degree of egotism and self-glorification. But most believed both implicitly and explicitly that men free to believe as they wished in a free state was the ideal to attain.

2.
Religious Influences on
Early American Documents

George Bancroft, the first accomplished American historian, said in 1835, with a deep and abiding belief in the "divine right" of America, that "The material world does not change in its masses or in its powers . . . The earth turns on its axis, and perfects its revolutions, and renews its seasons, without increase or advancement.

"But a like passive destiny does not attach to the inhabitants of the earth. . . . We have functions which connect us with heaven, as well as organs which set us in relation with earth. We have not merely the senses opening to us the external world, but an internal sense, which places us in connexion [sic] with the world of intelligence and the decrees of God." [1]

Such a sense existed in the fertile mind of Benjamin Franklin as he devised the ill-fated Albany Plan of Union of 1754. With Britain involved in a protracted struggle with France over control of Central, if not all of North America, the British colonies were, or would be to some degree, for better or worse, embedded in this conflict.

Britain had exercised what is often called "salutary neglect" over the colonies until the French Empire began to totter. It was at such a time that the Albany Conference was convened primarily to negotiate with the Iroquois Indians an important military alliance against the French.

The Albany Congress adopted a resolution which proposed some form of union of the colonies and that such an union was imperative for their preservation. At this point in the conference, Franklin presented his plan of union, which the congress adopted and then recommended to the assemblies of the various colonies. Franklin's Albany Plan was essentially a federal system of government within the British Empire. It foreshadowed the dominion scheme and, later, the British Commonwealth of Nations of the twentieth century. Some constitutional historians have suggested that adoption of Franklin's proposal would have averted the revolutionary conflict and perhaps indefinitely solved the controversy of imperial organization.

But Franklin's plan was doomed to failure. It was rejected by both the colonies and the British Crown for diametrically opposite reasons. The colonies were certain such a plan would reduce their local autonomy and increase British authority through a strong central government in America. The British, on the other hand, were convinced that it would consolidate too much power in the hands of the colonies and in turn increase colonial autonomy. The failure of the Albany Plan laid the groundwork for the conflict that was to emerge when the British government determined, after the Seven Years War, to reorganize British colonial patterns. It is fair to say that the attempted modifications by Britain directly precipitated the American Revolution.

In a certain sense, Benjamin Franklin's religion played a part in framing such a plan. The content of the Albany Plan of Union is consistent with his world view, and his belief (described in 1790 in a letter to Ezra Styles, a Congregational minister and president of Yale College) "that the most acceptable service we render to him [God, creator of the universe] is doing good to his other children." [2] Knowledge, not dogma, linked to responsibility was Franklin's creed.

Franklin indeed helped point the way toward the conception of federalism, which has become the great contribution of the American governmental system. The Articles of Confederation and the Constitution of the United States delegated to the federal government most of the powers proposed for the central government in Franklin's Albany Plan. Reason rather than revelation was the watchword for Franklin, and it manifested itself brilliantly in his creative Albany Plan of Union. Franklin, the moderate and prudent man, became the leader and, in a sense, one of the early spokesmen of the widely-held American view of the eighteenth century: "Reason is the arbiter of all truth, reason is the voice of God to man." [3]

The era of revolution in America from 1765 to 1776, at times and in retrospect, seemed inevitable, as though the disputants were determined to see and experience conflict. Yet at the same time, both American and British positions were claimed to be rooted in "divine right" under the Christian God, or at least in deistic fashion, an all-powerful creator God often called "Providence" or the "Infinite Power which rules the destinies of the Universe."

James Bryce, looking back in 1889, asserted that the American system of government "is the work of men who believed in original sin and were resolved to leave open for transgressors no door which they could possibly shut." [4] David Ramsey, a medical doctor and delegate from South Carolina to the Continental Congress, delivered an oration (1779) in which he is considerably more optimistic of the hopes and blessings of God. "We are laying the foundation of happiness for countless millions. . . . Oh glorious days! Oh kind, indulgent, bountiful Providence, that we live in this highly favoured period, and have the honour of helping forward these great events, and of suffering in a cause of such infinite importance." [5]

Between 1774 and 1776, in reaction to the oppression of Great Britain, the *de facto* governments of the various colonies passed into the hands of the revolutionists. By 1776, before the Declaration of Independence was even signed, the American colonies were in the process of becoming American states.

The First Continental Congress was conservative in tone with John Dickinson, John Jay, and Joseph Galloway urging caution and conciliation with Britain. A proposal similar to the Albany Plan of Union was proposed by Galloway and defeated by a single vote. Gradually, the extremist faction began to gain the upper hand. By the time of the Second Continental Congress in 1775, the tide of sentiment was moving toward a complete break with Britain. In 1776, there was no turning back, for *de facto* independence already existed, and it only remained necessary to make it formal and root it in law. In early July of that year, the Congress adopted the Declaration of Independence, which had been written by Thomas Jefferson.[6]

The Declaration of Independence was primarily intended for public consumption in order to rally support for the American revolution from France, among some in Britain, and many in America. Jefferson, as author of the Declaration of Independence, sought to portray four main political concepts: (1) the doctrine of natural law and natural right, (2) the compact theory of the state, (3) the view of popular sovereignty, and (4) the right of revolution. John Alden, in *A History of the American Revolution,* described the Declaration of Independence as "couched in solemn, dignified, felicitous and mellifluous language that remains impressive and alluring."[7]

For Jefferson and those who signed the Declaration, it was something much more. It was to be an inspiration to all Americans and a challenge to create a better human order, not only in America but around the world. In a sense, America assumed a divine mission. One author believed that the Revolution was similar to a Protestant revival, a struggle to gain the true Christian faith, and America herself became the instrument of the divine.[8] Jefferson himself was convinced that the Declaration would endure, for he believed only truth could stand by itself. Reason was paramount for Jefferson. Generally, he did not ascribe miraculous or religious attributes to the Declaration of Independence. Even years after the event, Jefferson stated that he did not compose something new but rather sought to place before men ideas that were clear and simple and command their acceptance.

Although religion did not seem to play a major role in the establishment and structuring of the Declaration of Independence, it was never far below the surface in the minds of leaders like Jefferson and Franklin. In 1776, both Jefferson and Franklin proposed designs of the Great Seal of the United States. Their designs portrayed Moses on the shore of the Red Sea with the pillar of fire shining upon him as he extended his hands over the water which was about to overwhelm Pharaoh and the Egyptians. The seal, proposed in the same year as the Declaration of Independence, would seem to imply that they both accepted some concept of God, be it only a deist God, who was somehow involved in human history and even in the American scene. The suggested motto illustrates this concept to an even greater degree, "Rebellion to tyrants is obedience to God." [9]

The Declaration itself contains only two references to God and then only of the most general kind. A reference in the first paragraph to "Nature's God" really only refers to the God-given rights of all men. The reference to "Divine Providence" in the last paragraph does point to an expectation or hope that a supernatural power, as well as the material commitment of the signers, will accomplish the ends of the Declaration.

One aspect of the Declaration of Independence that is often discussed from the religious point of view is the relationship of slavery to the phrase, "We hold these truths to be self-evident, that all men are created equal, that they are endowed by their Creator with certain unalienable Rights, that among these are Life, Liberty and the pursuit of Happiness." Jefferson, along with Washington and Madison, maintained the hope that slavery would be abolished eventually; because of the potential opposition from the Southern colonies, the concept of liberty in the Declaration was tacitly understood to exclude slavery. The hard realities of the economic system forced idealism into the background. Indentured servitude was considered in almost the same view, with little or no concern during the Revolutionary period to improve the lot of the indentured servant.

In this period, Americans were generally more concerned about prisoners and others who lost their freedom because of crime or debt. A number of societies were formed to help with improving prison conditions and alleviating harsh penalties for what we would now call "minor" crimes. The death penalty was regularly administered for such crimes as robbery, forgery, and burglary. As early as 1776, in Virginia, Jefferson attempted to apply "reason" to the criminal code and establish more humanitarian punishments by abolishing the death penalty for all offenses except treason and murder. Virginia did not act on these laws until 1796.

The Declaration of Independence set the stage for the revolution, but it was the successful war which confirmed it.

The first requirement after the Declaration of Independence was to formulate a regular government or governments. In June, 1776, before the Declaration of Independence was even passed, a five-member committee headed by John Dickinson produced a constitution for the "United Colonies." The document, conservative in nature and granting considerable authority to the central government, was unacceptable to the radical elements in the Congress. In late 1777, after considerable modification, the Articles of Confederation were submitted to the states for ratification and finally approved on March 1, 1781.

The shift in thrust of the religious orientation of the documents after the Declaration of Independence is obvious. The millennial hopes inherent in the Declaration of Independence, and which are so much a part of the Protestant dream, are missing from the Articles of Confederation and later the Constitution of the United States. Although there were many sermons in America's churches affirming the righteousness of the American cause, the documents themselves belie any strong religious thrust. Two interesting phenomena emerged in the period following the Declaration of Independence. The state constitutions, with some exceptions, determined to protect the states from democracy or the concept of the governed as spelled out in the Declaration. The new United States moved to a pattern which continues to the present—a concept of pragmatism in the formal arrangements of governmental structure. The Articles of Confederation were a prelude to the Constitutional Convention of 1787, which led in turn to the Constitution itself.

The Constitution did not provide much of a religious thrust or orientation. Article VI did provide that there could be no religious test for any public office of the United States. There were even some individuals who were less than enthusiastic for ratification of the constitution, because so little had been said about religion. It was certainly clear that the new government would not support a specific religion, but even as prominent an individual as Patrick Henry would have favored a moderate plan of governmental support for all religious groups. Baptists, and other groups would not support such a position, and it was decided that religion should be left outside the purview of government.

Once the Constitution was ratified, it was generally venerated by the citizens of America. The ratification process, however, did have some important religious aspects, particularly in Virginia and centered around the names of James Madison and John Leland. Opposition to the Constitution, often led by Baptists, had developed in the backcountry areas of Virginia. Much of the opposition was focused on the question of religious liberty. Leland, an articulate Baptist spokesman, opposed any organic union of church and state. He was convinced of the relationship between civil rights and religious rights. Leland was influential in, if not responsible for, the formulation of the First Amendment to the Constitution which stated in part, "Congress shall make no law respecting an establishment of religion or prohibiting the free exercise thereof. . . ." [10]

This Amendment has been the center of controversy from its earliest days. Initially, the question arose as to the proper terminology for the Amendment, since at least five states had an established church in some form. The question has been debated frequently since 1789. Just exactly what does "no law respecting an establishment of religion" mean? The concept of strict neutrality was accepted by some. That religion should be free from legal restrictions and from governmental encouragement and promotion was the view of others. The most rigid view of all was absolute separation of church and state. [11]

The Constitution and the Bill of Rights had given to churches, as Winthrop S. Hudson has pointed out, "the right to be completely self-governing," but also the obligation to "be completely self-supporting and self-perpetuating." [12] The voluntary aspect of the American church became most important to the later American scene. It presents an opportunity to propagate and remain close to the constituency, but also a challenge to lead the members to relevant and expanding faith. Accurately, it can be said emphatically, "The American principle of the separation of church and state as the constitutional basis for religious liberty has frequently and rightfully been called, 'America's greatest contribution to world civilization.' " [13]

3.
The Christian Impact on Early America

The origin of the Christian religion in America is directly related to the European explorers who visited the American shores probably beginning in the tenth century. These Norsemen apparently did not linger long nor generally establish colonies, but came primarily as fishermen.

The first continuing impact of the Christian religion on America began in the late fifteenth century with the explorations of the Spanish under Christopher Columbus and the English under John Cabot. The first expedition of Columbus was supported by Queen Isabella because her treasurer convinced her that the expedition "could prove of so great service to God and the exaltation of the Church not to speak of very great increase and glory for her realms and crown." [1]

After several months of negotiation, Columbus set sail on August 3, 1492. Seventy days later, he knelt on an island of the Bahamas, naming it San Salvador—Holy Savior. Although no priests went with Columbus on his first voyage, he took his religious obligations seriously. Vespers were conducted on each of his ships just after sunset. Prayers were said, a creed recited, and a Benedictine chant sung. On San Salvador, Columbus tried to make friendly contact with the Indians. He was convinced that they could be converted by love rather than force. Columbus himself believed that his success could be attributed not to his own merit but "to the holy Christian faith, and to the piety and religion of [his] Sovereigns." [2]

Explorations of the new world were conducted for a number of reasons, including profit and the love of God, but competition developed among several European countries. The Spanish were successful in exploring the area of Florida and other sections of the southern parts of the present United States. In most instances, these explorations were accompanied by Roman Catholic priests who often sought to convert the Indians they met. In a number of instances, these priests or missionaries were murdered by the very people they sought to serve. Many of the missionaries successfully established stations, and the missions begun among the Indians continued into permanent settlements. At times, the evangelistic methods used were ludicrous, as in the case where a priest or missionary would preach a message in his own language, declaring after the sermon that all the native inhabitants were to be baptized, thus becoming members of the established church. This practice enabled the churches to claim large numbers of converts, but did nothing to prevent extensive massacres of the Indians and conflicts between them and the Europeans.

The efforts of the French in attempting to establish colonies must also be remembered. Samuel de Champlain led explorations and established settlements along the coasts of present-day Maine. The later colonial settlements at Quebec and Montreal became the base for explorers who were also missionaries into the vast hinterland of the New World. Names like Marquette, Joliet, and La Salle are permanently embedded in the fabric of middle America. The Roman Catholic religion planted by the explorers remained for many years a vital part of the religious picture in the Mississippi Valley.

The English, one of the largest groups of explorers and those with which most Americans are familiar, made a profound religious impact upon the American scene. John Cabot, who sailed in the late 1400's, laid the English claim in the New World. Cabot's efforts and those of his son, Sebastian, however, should not be considered particularly great, but only the prelude to later English development. Sir Francis Drake left a notable legacy in the sixteenth century. Although Drake is best described as a pirate, he was an explorer and, like Columbus, religiously devout. Drake's religious devotion was linked to his English

Protestant heritage. Frequently, his pirate efforts against Spain were considered as blows against Catholicism and for Protestantism. It was a result of Drake's travels that Protestant religious services were first held in America.

The Roman Catholic religion was specifically fostered in the French and Spanish areas of America by most of their explorers. It was common for them to assert that their success depended entirely upon the will and favor of God. Most of these explorers had a Catholic priest who traveled with them to meet the spiritual needs of the expedition and to serve as missionaries to the Indians as well. Among those who worked with and for the Spanish was Father Mark who traveled north from Mexico City in 1539 to the northern portions of Arizona and New Mexico, claiming for the King of Spain all the areas he visited.

Although the Spaniards supported the work of the priests, and the priests, in turn, the Spanish authority, all was not well with Spanish-Indian relationships. Most of the conquistadors, in their all-consuming quest for gold, sought to subjugate, enslave, and abuse the Indians. Bartholomew Las Casas, the first priest ordained in the New World, sought to alleviate excessive abuse against the Indians. Armed with the title, "Defender of the Indians," he tried to do what he could for their cause. After almost twenty years of work, however, he was forced to acknowledge failure. Although freedom was not always achieved by the Indian, at least the presence of the missionaries usually modified the political and social climate toward a more humane stance.

Many of the seventeenth century explorations by the French into the Mississippi Valley were led by Roman Catholic priests and missionaries such as Jean de Brebeuf, Jacques Marquette, and others. These missionaries and their religious orders left a lasting mark on the Indians, and their presence was felt for generations.

The explorations of the English, and the areas they came to dominate on the Eastern coast of America, left a deep influence on the religious milieu of early America. While it is true that the Dutch, Swedes, Germans, and English were often mixed together in the early history of America, it is really the English who left the deepest religious imprint.

Any survey of the religious life of the New World will reveal that the religious patterns were derived directly from Europe. W. W. Sweet has suggested that one of the distinctive marks of religion in the New World is that the churches of colonial America were established by religious radicals.[3] Winthrop Hudson further indicates that the terms *English* and *Protestant* used in America explain the desire of the colonists for liberty, but also the degree both of diversity and unity which exists in American Protestantism.[4] It is also fair to say that many who came to America were independent individualists in the area of religion.

The stage was set for English Protestant religion in the New World through the extensive writings of Richard Hakluyt. Hakluyt portrayed in his work, without apology, that the rulers of England, who had the title, "Defender of the Faith," should evangelize through exploration in order to lift "the poor people" who had been so long in darkness. Many Englishmen heeded and supported this religious cause, but it would be naive to ignore the lure of worldly possessions as another powerful motivating force to emigrate to the New World.

The sixteenth century was not an especially prosperous period for English colonies in America. Almost without exception, all the attempted ventures at colonizing failed dismally. The seventeenth century, on the other hand, began the floodtide in which the English came to dominate the American scene.

There are two distinct strains, with possibly one additional, from which the America of the eighteenth century was born. The earliest was the settlement of Jamestown in 1607 in what is now Virginia. This English colony was established through the efforts of the London Company which had been granted a charter to the area of Virginia. The London Company had a number of prominent English people among its shareholders. These individuals influenced the company to pursue a colonization policy which sought to perpetuate and advance the established Protestant Church of England. In a certain sense, this support for the Church of England was an attempt to duplicate the pattern of Spain, which supported the advancement of the Roman Catholic Church through its colonial policy. Although it would be a gross overstatement to say that the colony in Virginia was established for religious reasons, it is important to remember that one of the colony's early leaders, John Rolfe— who is perhaps best remembered for his marriage to the Indian princess, Pocahontas—believed that Englishmen had been "chosen by the finger of God" to establish the colony. He was equally sure that God would bless their efforts.

The first religious emphases in this colony were led by Robert Hunt, the chaplain to the first colonists. Hunt was reportedly a most effective and respected clergyman, for he was successful in resolving conflicts between various groups in the colonies by what one observer called "good doctrine and exhortation." The total efforts of this dedicated leader are not known. He apparently died in 1608, the victim of the privations of the frontier. The colony continued and, despite difficulties in the early years, survived.

The establishment of the Church of England along the same patterns as in the mother land did not go well in America. The simple problem of distance and lack of population in the New World made parishes very large, and, coupled with the critical shortage of clergymen, resulted in variations of religious practice. A colonist was often without the services of a clergyman at the times in his life when he most needed one.

In a religious sense, necessity became the mother of invention. The small family cemeteries often supplanted the church burial ground. The problems between the clergy and laity increased in the seventeenth and early eighteenth centuries. The support provided to the clergy in Virginia was limited, and that, in turn, sometimes led to inferior clergymen arriving in Virginia from England. Another handicap was the lack of a place in Virginia to train Virginians for the ministry. Furthermore, the lack of a bishop in America was also a difficulty, for it meant that all matters of discipline had to be referred to England. Such a circumstance resulted in the Anglican church's being ruled in America virtually along congregational lines, rather than episcopal.

It is too simplistic to suggest that these facts would explain the rise and growth of the churches with a congregational form of church government, but these facts should not be overlooked. H. Richard Niebuhr suggests that the Protestant in America, regardless of heritage, was aware of modifications of his creed and polity which had been produced as a result of interaction with other religious groups and with the "democratic, scientific, and industrial civilization." [5]

The second, and most important, early religious influence on America was tied to the Puritans. There are many splendid studies of the Puritans and their early and continuing impact upon America. It is helpful to summarize simply and briefly some aspects of this important heritage in the religious beginnings of America. Perry Miller observes that the people of the Puritan colonies, at least Massachusetts and Connecticut, conceived of themselves as a chosen race and entered into a specific relationship with God. The prosperity or calamity that befell them was directly related to divine action and was never interpreted as the result of natural or impersonal forces. [6]

In 1620, a group of English religious pilgrims left Leyden in Holland, where they had lived for a number of years, to go to the New World. Because one of their ships foundered, they landed instead in England. The religious climate was still not hospitable to them, so they sailed westward on the *Mayflower* a second time. The pilgrims had arranged to enter the area of Virginia, but their ship was blown off course, so they were forced to settle in New England. The pilgrims had neither the authorization to land in New England nor the basis for a suitable system of government once they did settle there. They devised the famous Mayflower Compact, an agreement among the participants, drawn up along the lines of a voluntary church covenant. This Compact established the structure of government of what became known as the Plymouth Colony until 1691, when it was united with the larger Massachusetts Bay Colony.

While the Plymouth Colony is often studied and considered the bellwether of Puritanism in New England, it was the Massachusetts Bay Colony which actually shaped the destiny of Puritanism. Historians have frequently debated as to what percentage of the early settlers were sympathetic to the religious views of the leaders. Whatever the case may be, it is true that the leaders put a profound Puritan imprint upon the government, religion, culture, social life, and family patterns of New England. Alice Felt Tyler says, "Their philosophy was based upon the Calvinistic ideas of the Puritans and the teachings of the great English theorists of the Parliamentary revolt of the seventeenth century, who had emphasized the importance of the individual and his union with other individuals in organizations based upon mutual consent." [7]

There is a certain sense in which Puritanism was the first wave of European influence upon America. In some respects, it gave as lasting an impact as any of the voices which came later. The early Puritans of America, influenced and permeated as they were with Calvinism, tended toward republicanism and democracy as they are known today. It is really not at all surprising that Calvinism, even among those who had some established church ties in England, tended in New England to become established Congregationalism. In New England there developed what in both the religious and political spheres is properly called "Dynamic Democracy," according to Tyler.

Although many of the Puritans came to America seeking religious liberty, it was not long until they, too, became the establishment and began to suppress religious liberty. Gaustad suggests that one should not be too critical of these Puritans, for they came to America for "their own liberty, not all men's liberty." [8] In a real sense, the Puritan leaders sought to establish a "noble experiment" which, while in form differed from the Utopian schemes of the nineteenth century, was not dissimilar from their goal of a community guided by what they believed was the rule of God. It was imperative for them, as it had been for their earlier persecutors, to maintain the purity of the religion.

It is interesting that, despite the attempts at uniformity in religion in early America, the individualism of the colonists welled up and led to new calls for freedom. As the French observer De Tocqueville was to remark a century later, in America the spirit of religion and the spirit of freedom reigned hand-in-hand. The concept of individual freedom was concomitant with the concept of exile. In America, the religious individualist was determined to move ahead with his own views, but at the same time, because of the broad expanse of uninhabited territory, the easiest solution for the established society was the exile of those with deviant religious views toward the frontier.

The first major example of religious exile in America was the expulsion of Roger Williams from Massachusetts. Regarded by some as the godfather and architect of the later American concept of separation of church and state, Williams was the prophet of complete religious liberty. Williams believed that for the Christian faith to be genuine, it must be free and voluntary. When in the winter of 1635-36 he was exiled from Salem, Massachusetts, he went to Providence and after some effort, including a trip to England, he received a charter for the Rhode Island colony. Rhode Island became the first modern state to separate religious matters from the civil authority and guarantee complete religious liberty.

Although it would be far from the truth to say that religious liberty was accepted in all the colonies of early America, it would be fair to say that by the middle of the eighteenth century, religious toleration was generally accepted in every English area. Perry Miller, the astute observer of the colonial scene, notes that the Protestants of early America stumbled into religious liberty only by compulsion, and finally only accepted it because they had to, and only then saw its "strategic value." [9]

There is a sense in which the desire for religious liberty in America was merged with the pragmatic realities of the economic and social situation. Peter Stuyvesant, the governor of New

Netherlands, tried to suppress the Jews, Quakers, and others. He wanted to keep them out of New Amsterdam. But the directors of the Dutch West India Company reminded him that everyone in the colony should be unmolested and free—as long as they were modest and did not infringe upon others. There are other examples that illustrate a move toward greater religious toleration such as those in Maryland and the middle colonies.

The religious patterns of the colonial period should not be viewed as only a struggle between absolute, authoritarian, established religion on the one hand, and free, secularized, religious anarchy on the other. Many within the established churches did move to a deep theologically significant religion in what is known as the Great Awakening. This revival of religion in the eighteenth century followed a period called by Cedric B. Cowing "The Glacial Age." [10] This First Great Awakening has been studied and discussed from many perspectives. Its effects were profound from the development of the first truly American theology in the life and teachings of Jonathan Edwards to, as W. W. Sweet describes, "a new social consciousness and broad humanitarianism, which manifested itself in a greater concern for the poor and the alleviation of distress and suffering." [11] Sydney Mead suggests that there was also a merging of the traditional European patterns of church and sect which manifested itself in new organizational structures which are called in America, "denominations." [12]

Religiously, the Colonial period in America was the prelude to the advances and changes which affected the new country for many generations. The reaction to and acceptance of religious ideas in the next two centuries prompts an American of the twentieth century to ask the question: was the Christianization of America achieved before the Revolution, or after? Or, then again, has it ever been achieved at all?

4.
The Christianization of America Achieved?

A question which presents itself to Christians in twentieth-century America is: has the Christianization of America been achieved? Winfred Garrison suggests that the church throughout its history has experienced two profound revolutions. The first of these was in the fourth century when the church ceased to be a voluntary body and became integrally linked with society as a necessary adjunct to it. The second was the situation in America when the reverse took place, and the church and the society were separated.[1] Thomas Jefferson declared that the first amendment to the Constitution of the United States established "a wall of separation between the church and the state."[2]

Despite the separation between church and state, and the acceptance of the belief that the civil authority should be neutral and impartial regarding religious faith, it would be a gross overstatement to suggest that religion and the church never affected or Christianized the society. As the first two chapters have shown, religion did indeed play a part in the formation of the new country. There have been numerous other ways in which the church and religion sought to capture the minds of Americans. It is faulty to suggest that the religious bodies in America influenced the people and the culture uniformly or in a monolithic manner. R. Morton Darrow in his essay, *The Church and Techniques of Political Action,* asserts that in a federal system of government like the United States of America, the distribution of membership of any religious body is of equal importance with its size.[3]

The majority of the churches in America assumed particular responsibility to "proclaim liberty throughout all the land unto all the inhabitants thereof," especially during what was known as the Great Awakening. In the beginning, many churches, including most Baptist churches, opposed the Great Awakening as too emotional. Several denominations, including the Presbyterians and Congregationalists, actually were divided between those who favored the revivals and those who opposed them. Despite their opposition, the Baptists were the group who benefitted most during the following decades.

The Great Awakening as an outgrowth of evangelical pietism exerted a profound influence upon America, particularly at the time of the American Revolution. Mead believed that the Revolutionary Era marked the turning point in the history of Christianity in America.[4] Cowing suggests that immediately following the end of the Great Awakening, c. 1750, there was a wider acceptance of French ideas related to rationalism in America, and even the pietists cooperated limitedly with the rationalists and their views, even if only long enough to secure new religious freedoms.[5]

William G. McLoughlin goes even further by saying that the evangelical revivals and movement laid the foundation for the American Revolution. "Experimental piety [of the Great Awakening and the revivals] was . . . the completion of deistic rationalism in capturing the minds of enlightened Americans. It stated in religious terms what the Enlightenment philosophers wanted to state primarily in humanistic, secular or rationalistic terms." [6]

In a real sense, during this period, the common people of America accepted evangelical pietism, not because it was especially reasonable, but because it worked and seemed to offer a sense of purpose and meaning. The proclamation of its message sometimes produced immediate and, what some would call self-evident, modifications and results. Cowing goes so far as to state: "It seems clear that without the large evangelical component in the colonial population, there would have been no military victory over the redcoats, and beyond that no Independence, no Constitution, no legalized religious freedom, and no dramatic opportunity to be a beacon to the world." [7]

On the parallel side, however, there was often a haziness among the common man as to what kind of faith was important. Frequently, they wanted their fellows to be consciously committed to religious and pious action, while at the same time believing that fixed creeds restricted godliness and inhibited individuality. It was true in both the eighteenth and early nineteenth centuries, not to mention the twentieth century, when a veneer of religiosity was considered good and profitable in the business and political spheres of America. One often heard the words of God but saw the actions of mammon coming from the same source—and if not at the same time, at least so close together that it was difficult, if not impossible, to discern when one left off, and the other began. The story of religion and the American experience in the eighteenth and early nineteenth centuries was appropriately, as Tyler termed it, "Freedom's Ferment."

Perhaps the most pivotal religious effect upon the new republic was the acceptance of religious liberty and the complete separation of church and state. Roger Williams of Rhode Island, mentioned in the previous chapter, was responsible more than any other person for the launching of this revolutionary idea. Williams had based his philosophy of religious liberty on great fundamental truths and was willing to, and did undergo, danger and hardship for the cause of complete religious liberty. John Callender, pastor of the First Baptist Church of Newport, Rhode Island, from 1731 to 1748, preached his "Century Sermon" in 1738, which celebrated the history of Rhode Island and of the Baptists there. In his century sermon, he stated that before the coming of Williams and John Clarke, founder of the Baptist church at Newport, Rhode Island, the true grounds of liberty of conscience were not understood in America.[8]

Of all the denominations in American history, the Baptists can, without doubt, lay claim to consistent and usually enthusiastic support of the concept of complete religious freedom and its corollary, the separation of church and state. Many historians and theologians have described the Baptist stance on religious liberty as their greatest contribution to Christianity and American civilization.[9] "In historical perspective, . . . it has not simply been the proclamation of religious liberty but the *exercise* of religious liberty that has been the concern of Baptists." [10]

In the seventeenth century, Baptists of various theological persuasions articulated their beliefs in religious liberty, but, at most, they can be described as a small band of believers crying in the wilderness and apparently, on the basis of persecutions inflicted, seldom heard. David Benedict points out that in Massachusetts, Baptists suffered more than in any other state in the union at the hands of recalcitrant secular leaders determined to maintain "their legal sacro-secular establishment." [11]

Prior to the Great Awakening and the Revolution, Baptists were not only a small religious body but "were considered religious radicals of the most dangerous type, and were frequently looked upon as enemies of all political and social order." [12] It was the struggle of Baptists during and before the Revolutionary period that provided complete religious freedom for all citizens. This was the period when Baptists truly came of age. The movement of many Separates—who had been linked with the established Congregational church and then became separate—into the Baptist fold assisted this development.[13] Isaac Backus of Massachusetts became an articulate spokesman of Baptists in that area for religious liberty and even appeared before the Continental Congress to urge freedom of religion for all citizens as a part of the redress of grievances against Britain.

It remained, however, for John Leland, a Baptist minister from Virginia, to provide the spark which ignited Virginia to disestablish the state church and the new country to adopt the Bill of Rights as amendments to the United States Constitution. The first amendment, as has been noted earlier, prohibited Congress from passing any laws respecting the establishment of religion.[14] The Baptist position that religious liberty was fundamental to all liberties had come to be accepted by the United Staes of America.

The American Revolution also affected profoundly what are called the "Free churches," Baptists particularly, and to a lesser degree Methodists and Presbyterians. Their almost universal support for the American cause—and emphasis upon the individual and the individual congregation, as well as adherence to the concept of democratic rights in their churches—enabled them to make a large and growing appeal to the common people.

While it is true that there was a real declension in religion during and immediately following the Revolution, the struggle for religious liberty did encourage the Baptists and Methodists in particular to develop a national spirit. Both of these groups did not actually have an "official" national organization until after the Revolution.

In the early part of the nineteenth century, the impact of revivalistic concepts played and continued to play a decisive role in religious life in America. The growth experienced by most of what are considered today the mainline denominations in America was phenomenal. The United States was fertile soil for the churches, but only those who deliberately sought to reach the unredeemed were successful. Some observers have emphasized that when the common man is freed from political absolutism, he will seek to relieve himself of theological absolutism.

In the early nineteenth century, a religious awakening took place in the older sections of the country, as well as on the frontier. The revivals on the frontier, sometimes called the Second Great Awakening, positively affected Baptists and Methodists most.[15] These revivals should never be viewed as simply frontier phenomena because most, if not all, of the leadership of the revivals was influenced by or originated in the Eastern Seaboard regions.

As the settlers moved across the mountains, they were separated from the eastern churches. It would have appeared that the Presbyterians and Congregationalists, with the largest number of migrants moving westward, would have fared best, but both these groups insisted upon an educated clergy. The appeal of these groups to the frontiersmen was usually less than that of the Baptists and Methodists. The Roman Catholics were served by itinerant priests, but their numbers were small. The church relied on the influx of immigrants from the Catholic countries of Europe to enlarge their ministry and communicants. Many visitors to the west observed that there were very few Episcopalians on the frontier.

The uniqueness of the leadership for Baptists was that the typical preacher came from the ranks of the people with whom he lived. He was a farmer during the week, except when pastoral duties called him to preach, and a preacher on Sunday. Frequently, although not always, he had little formal education, and some even prided themselves on their lack of education. Newman states that Baptists often were suspicious of the educated preacher and preferred one who supported himself by secular pursuits.[16] There is little doubt that the simplicity of their doctrine, the democracy of their organization, their ability to propagate themselves without overhead machinery, and their appeal to the common men all contributed to the rapid growth of Baptists. The doctrine of believers' baptism also kept them unique from the other evangelical groups with which they frequently cooperated "to reach the lost."

The Methodists were most vigorous in their work on the frontier and soon in many areas became the largest religious group. The organizational structure of the Methodist church was autocratic and centralized, but under their first American Bishop, Francis Asbury, an extensive network of circuit-riding evangelists was organized. Methodist doctrine also lent itself to the frontier because it, too, was democratic in emphasizing a gospel of free will and free grace, each man being equal before the Lord. Each individual needed to experience a religious conversion, and the suggestion that Methodism was the "creedless religion of the heart" is appropriate. The life of the frontier circuit rider was hard and demanding, but he was helped by laymen who were encouraged to exercise their gifts by attending established Methodist classes and accepting licenses to preach. The Methodist circuit riders as well as the other leadership of the church travelled extensively to be where the people were and minister to them wherever and whenever they could.

To explain the growth and effectiveness of Baptists and Methodists on the frontier is in many respects complex. The need for the righteous influence of the church was clearly evident in the National Period when the religious and moral conditions of our nation reached their lowest ebb.[17] Although conditions had sunk to such a low point in the settled areas, the situation was even worse in the sparsely-settled regions of the West, where few external restraints existed. The frontier areas needed the churches which became the moral courts of that society.[18]

Despite all that has been said about the apparent anti-intellectualistic position of Baptists and other groups in the early National Period, the revival movement greatly advanced American education. Baptists, along with Presbyterians and Methodists, led out in establishing permanent colleges during this period, and Congregationalists, Roman Catholics and Episcopalians were not far behind.[19]

The question still remains: has the Christianization of America been achieved? Crime is on the increase, dishonesty and what might be called "sub-honesty" are ever-present. The total attendance on any given Sunday in American churches usually does not equal half the membership. Despite the surge of "piety" in the 1950's and 1960's, many do not ever, or seldom, enter any church. Even though during the twentieth century, more people in America belong to a church than ever before, the problems remain, the injustices continue to fester.

The purpose of this chapter has been to trace the major high points of victory or achievements by the religious forces in America. The major victories over clear-cut religious issues should not be overshadowed by other improvements. It is true in America that every conceivable pattern, trend, and ideal in religion have been noticed. John L. Eighmy's statement with reference to Southern Baptists could probably be applied to most religious groups in America. They "have responded to social issues more significantly than is generally recognized."[20] The editor of Eighmy's work, Samuel S. Hill, Jr., raises a valid point in his preface. Hill stresses that any study concerning the social involvements of religious groups often must rest on the available historical sources, which in many cases are the official statements of the group or denomination under study. Hill is most correct in asserting that there is often a considerable difference "between what is preached-promoted by the professional leadership and what is perceived by the masses of members." [21]

A similar situation exists in the realm of religion and politics in America. Regarding several articles in *Religious Perspectives in American Culture,* Smith and Jamison state that "the bearing of religion on political action has been highly ambiguous, seldom clearly defined, and never entirely effective. . . . The tension between the ideal and the actual, between the extended and the achieved, is never quite resolved." [22] They conclude with a most positive statement. "It is possible that such tension is a continuing mark of the vitality of a civilized society." [23]

There have been definite occasions in the history of America when modification and change occurred in the society because of, and sometimes in spite of, the role of religion. It is most difficult to assert regarding many of these events that "religion" was the deciding factor. There is a sense in which religion played a part in the ending of negro slavery and the establishing of civil rights legislation.[24] Prison reform, child labor laws, and women's rights are also examples of when the church spoke with vigor against such abuses in society.

There is a real sense in which dichotomy exists in America in the area of religion and culture. The voluntary principle in religion has prompted many individuals to be linked to the church. On the other hand, crusades and reforms often have come, not from the institutional religious structures, but from individuals who have believed in a specific action that they have considered necessary. These reformers have often been related directly or indirectly to a religious group. What may appear to be an "areligious" or secular project or concept may, in fact, be a devout expression of a real and vital faith. De Tocqueville was correct in saying that when he tried to find the genius of American institutions, he looked everywhere in vain, and did not find it until he entered the church. " 'It was there,' he said, 'as I listened to the soul-elevating principles of the gospel of Christ as they fell from Sabbath to Sabbath upon the masses of the people, that I learned why America was great and free, and why France was a slave.' " [25]

The Christianization of America may still be in the process of being achieved as the result of the ministry of the "unlikely." During the Civil Rights struggle of the 1950's and 1960's, bus boycotts frequently occurred. One boycott began when a black woman refused to yield her seat on a city bus to a white man who boarded after she did. Later, when she was asked why she did what she did, she replied, "I guess I was just tired." There are countless such examples when unexpected individuals with religious convictions have influenced the American experience.

In the twentieth century, as American churches became increasingly successful, they had to guard against being compromised or even absorbed by the surrounding culture. The problem, as America faces her two hundredth birthday, remains to preserve carefully the traditional allegiance to the separation of church and state which exists in America. A "cultural religion" carelessly merging a pseudo-patriotism with a quasi-patriotism must be avoided.

Basil (330-379 A.D.), in his *Address to Youth,* urges Christians, in relationship to the use and value of pagan literature, to be like a honeybee who passes from one flower to another, examining, perhaps even touching, but accepting only what is profitable, and rejecting what is unacceptable. The American scene has been influenced and sometimes dominated by religious forces. Religious pluralism has meant each religious group is a minority, and consequently the impact of religion on American culture has not been uniform or monolithic.

Christianization of America? "Blessed is the nation whose God is the Lord" (Psalm 33:12). The third century beckons America. "If this nation is to provide the political leadership and spiritual leadership which the world needs, America must become more Christian than ever in the past." [26]

"If we expect to win victories for Him in lands afar, . . . we must make our own land a demonstration station, revealing the triumph of Christianity by enthroning Christ in the life of our land." [27]

5.
Religion Modified by American Society

Since the Christian is to be in the world but not of it, the individual Christian and the Christian community must always maintain a critical attitude toward the state and its civil religion. Christians cannot get out of civil responsibilities. They must live in a constant state of tension with the world and its institutions. Sydney Mead said, "Church members in America have always been faced with the necessity to choose, implicitly at least, between the inclusive religion of democracy and the particular Christianity of their sect." [1]

One is tempted, in trying to deal with the subject of religion modified by American society and the Americanization of Christianity, to write a lament. To lament is to cry at the death or dying of someone or something loved. "In a lament for a child's death, there is not only pain and regret but also celebration of passed good." [2] One is tempted either to lament for a Christianity or religion that existed before it was changed by America, or to praise the religion or "Christianity" that has been improved by America. In this chapter an attempt will be made to examine religion and Christianity in the light of the American experience. We must be careful as we study this subject that we do not assume that our ideals and views are synonymous with the will of God, or that our foes or opponents are one with the devil.

As we have noted previously, American religion is a derivative of the Bible and of European Christianity. On the other hand, America has produced its particular variations, emphases, and nuances stimulated by the American environment and at times appears to have made this Christianity its own. The concept of the "free" church found in America was profoundly different from anywhere else. The isolated continent and the apparent unlimited frontier made it virtually impossible for any establishment to enforce its will against the wishes of the dissident.

It is true for religion in America that the frontier served as a safety valve, but in turn produced a pluralistic religious phenomenon. This pluralism was also amplified by the almost continuous stream of immigrants from abroad. American religion, then, is not only pluralistic but also generally voluntaristic, individualistic, democratic, pragmatic, activistic, revivalistic, and enthusiastic. The socio-political situation of America permitted and still permits almost every type of religious expression. In America, men and women have searched out reasons for their predecided position, such as the slaveholders of the South who used biblical texts to defend the institution of slavery. On the other hand, religion has been used as the basis for men to break through the barriers of custom, sometimes at considerable cost, to do "God's Will." J. Franklin Jameson, speaking before the American Historical Association in 1907, said, "Of all the means of estimating the American character . . . the pursuit of religious history is the most complete." [3]

A. Leland Jamison suggests that there are few areas of the world which have produced such wide religious proliferation in the last three centuries as has America. He offers a preliminary explanation that exploration and immigration, along with the mobility of American society, have prompted a wide diversification of religious views and institutions. The number of groups is difficult to determine because some are loosely organized, at times secret, and often only quasi-religious. If one were to attempt listing these groups which have grown up and perished during the course of American history, the number would be ever larger. [4]

Jamison offers these hints as to why America has received so many religious groups. (1) It is the consequence of religious freedom. (2) It is a symptom of cultural malaise and socio-religious anarchy. (3) It is an indication of religious vitality. [5] The choice of explanations is dependent upon the viewpoint of the questioner, and each contains some truth. The fact remains that religious pluralism does exist in America and is likely to continue. It is also important to notice that all religious groups in America are a minority, and each group has equal legal standing.

H. Richard Niebuhr, in his *The Social Sources of Denomi-nationalism,* suggests that the sect groups, i.e., those groups which demand some definite form of religious experience to gain admittance, often find their roots among the outcast minority, the disinherited, disadvantaged, and frequently, the poor.[6] These are not just the economically deprived but also the culturally and socially deprived. It is a reasonable assumption that the conventional churches often tend to become formalized and leave little room for religious spontaneity. Also, they are made up of people predisposed to justify the existing order of society. They tend to believe that the successful seem to evidence God's blessing, while the unsuccessful do not. It should not be surprising that the unsuccessful (by American standards) tend to withdraw, either abandoning religion or becoming part of the fringe groups.

One of the earliest native American "deviations" was seen in Anne Hutchinson, a radical spiritualist who claimed direct divine inspiration to discern the truth of God. The court of Massachusetts ruled that she should be cast out of the church and declared both a heathen and a leper, who should be withdrawn from the fellowship. The tension between direct and corporate revelation was really the point of issue.

In the eighteenth century, fewer groups originated in America than in any other era. There were several monastic-type groups of German pietists which emerged in the Pennsylvania area, such as the Hermits or Mystics, under the leadership of Johannes Kelpius and the Ephrata Community near Lancaster, led by Conrad Beissel. These two groups were really American manifestations of European patterns.

Although several of the major religious bodies in America divided in the eighteenth century over the First Great Awakening, few of the disputants developed a unique or completely different religious persuasion.

Such was not the case in the nineteenth century, however. Many deviations came into being—to make up, as it were, for lost time. Edwin Gaustad notes that following the American Revolution, when freedom was in the air, religious forces had to try their wings of freedom.[7]

Several groups emerged in what are called utopian experiments. Some of these groups were convinced that perfection would be the climax of a sure and steady progress. Others looked for a utopia that was a return to the purer days of the past. Both types of groups believed that the ideal society could be formed on earth.

It seemed by the nineteenth century that the problems which defied solution could now be solved. Politically, the impossible had happened—the strongest country in the world had been brought to her knees and had pulled her troops out of America. Why could not such a victory be achieved in religion?

Among the utopian schemes that flourished in the nineteenth century, and then waned, were the Rappite communities of New Harmony, Indiana, and Economy, Pennsylvania; the Oneida Community led by John Humphrey Noyes in Oneida, New York; and the Brook Farm Community of New England transcendentalists. All these were economically successful, but soon they dwindled in numbers. Among the more ecstatic were the Shakers of "Mother" Ann Lee who prospered for a time, but eventually declined because of their opposition to the mingling of the sexes in any way.[8]

Whitney R. Cross in the *Burned Over District* suggested that the area of Western New York was a microcosm of the entire country. This area was inhabited in early 1800 by New Englanders who had migrated westward. The New England stock was not monolithic, for the Congregational monopoly of religion had been broken, and there were a number of dissenters among the immigrants. Among this group, displaced people from the East, there were many who were inclined toward " 'eccentricity of opinion and extremity of temper.' " [9]

One of the most completely indigenous of all American religious movements and, up to the present, one of the successful was that founded in 1830 by Joseph Smith, Jr. Cross says that the "fundamental condition leading to the beginnings of Mormonism was the credulity and spiritual yearning which made people anxious to follow a prophet, whoever he might be." [10] Although Mormonism began in western New York, it left its deepest mark on the western United States. W. W. Sweet says, "No religious body in America has had a more bizarre origin than have the Mormons, and none has used its history so advantageously in creating loyalty and devotion among its members." [11]

Joseph Smith came of a family of "frontier nomads" who were frequently interested in the supernatural. The members of the Smith family attended the various revival services in the community and were members of different churches. Joseph, Jr., at a young age claimed to have seen visions beginning first in 1820. Smith alleged that an angel, Moroni, visited him and told him that the Bible of the New World was buried nearby, but it should not be touched until the angel gave special permission. In 1827, Smith is supposed to have received that permission and unearthed the golden plates and two crystals that acted as spectacles enabling him to translate what he described as "the reformed Egyptian tongue" into English. A small company of believers established themselves first at Kirtland Hills, Ohio, until they experienced difficulty with the authorities and consequently moved on to Missouri.

Again community pressures forced them to move in 1840, this time to Nauvoo, Illinois. The town was carefully planned and a Mormon temple built. In fact, Nauvoo became the largest city in Illinois.

A serious conflict again developed with neighbors when it became known that Smith had received a revelation which permitted Mormon males under certain circumstances to have more than one wife. In 1843 and 1844, the situation in Nauvoo deteriorated dramatically. A minor rebellion against Joseph Smith occurred, and the state militia was called to suppress the uprising. Smith and his brother, Hyrum, were arrested and taken to the county seat in Carthage, Illinois, and jailed. In June, 1844, an angry mob stormed the jail, and both were brutally murdered. It appeared that another utopian bubble had burst, but Brigham Young assumed leadership and lead the majority of the "Latter Day Saints" away from Illinois, first to Omaha, then on to the "Promised Land" of the Salt Lake Valley. Soon this area attracted large numbers of immigrants and, despite impossible odds, one utopian scheme in America survived. Some of the "saints" did not follow Young but remained behind, claiming to be the true continuing organization. Another smaller group went to Michigan, but the Reorganized Church of Jesus Christ of Latter Day Saints was organized in Missouri.

Certainly, Mormon doctrine was uniquely American and blended well with nineteenth-century ideas on the frontier. The theology was optimistic in its relationship to America, and Mormon piety glorified hard work and offered materialistic well-being in the present.

Only two other indigenous American religious groups will be discussed. The teaching of William Miller of Vermont became an extreme interpretation of millennialism. The premillennial view holds that Christ will return for a one-thousand year reign on earth when conditions here have become hopeless. The postmillennial view holds that as the world becomes prepared for Christ's reign, he will return for a thousand-year reign.

The former group is pessimistic; the latter, optimistic. Usually premillennialism prevails in troubled and chaotic times. The premillennial teachings of William Miller began in the 1830's in western New York and reached a high point as the country experienced serious financial depression in the panic of 1837. Miller was licensed to preach by a Baptist church and was much in demand as a speaker throughout the New York area. In 1836, he wrote a book made up of sixteen lectures entitled *Evidence from Scripture and History of the Second Coming of Christ, about the Year 1843.* His fame spread, and in 1839 he met Joshua Hines, pastor of the Chardon Street Baptist Church, Boston, who accepted Miller's millennial views and helped to disseminate them through a number of Adventist newspapers. Hines became Miller's promotion man and set the stage for what has been described as a "stupendous revival."

Miller never set an exact date for the coming of the Lord, but between February 28 and April 1, a bright comet appeared on the horizon which amplified the faith of the faithful. October 22, 1844, became the accepted date by most "Millerites" of the date of the Lord's return. The secular press indicated that mob scenes occurred in many major cities as the expected date arrived. The movement had a profound effect on many Baptist churches, some of which became Adventist congregation churches. When the Lord did not return, many Millerite followers gravitated back to their former churches, but surprisingly, the Advent movement continued. Miller interpreted the situation as merely an error in calculation. In 1861, the Adventist Christian Association was formed, which differed from the regular denominations only in its strong emphasis on the Advent doctrine. A second group led by Hiram Edson established the Seventh-day Adventists. Edson claimed a personal revelation that actually the Lord had come in heaven on October 22, 1844. The Seventh-day Adventists are noted today for the largest per capita financial giving of any religious group in America.

Another religious group that had its beginnings in America emerged in the 1860's but is really more closely related to the urban centers than to the frontier. Christian Science has sometimes been described as the religion of the prosperous. Mrs. Mary Baker Eddy, who had suffered from a nervous malady from her youth, had tried a number of physicians and possible cures, but all failed. She went to "Dr." P. P. Quimby in Portland, Maine, who was reported to have achieved some remarkable cures by methods of mental healing. Mrs. Eddy was healed and began to follow his teachings. She was even allowed to copy some of his manuscripts and used them after his death in 1866 in the interests of mental healing. In 1875, she wrote the Christian Science textbook, *Science and Health, with key to the Scriptures.* The Christian Science movement grew and was based on the teaching that matter has no real existence, nor has evil, sickness, sin, or even death. Disease is a product of the mind and can be cured in direct proportion as the mind is able to dispel a belief in disease. Such a state is achieved when the mortal mind is in harmony with the Eternal Mind as revealed in Jesus Christ.

The success or growth of Mormonism and Christian Science in the twentieth century may be related to Niebuhr's assertion in 1929 that "the mind and self-centered type of faith had become the real, if not always openly professed, religion of 'a bourgeoisie whose conflicts are over and which had passed into the quiet waters of assured income and established standing.' " [12] They have also survived and grown in the age of anxiety. This may be explained through a widespread spiritual hunger which is coupled with the American dream of material prosperity.

6.
Americanization of Christianity: Victory or Defeat?

Martin E. Marty in the preface to his unique book, *The Pro and Con Book of Religious America: A Bicentennial Argument*, states his belief that if people can live with contradiction and paradox, they are able to learn more from extremes in national life. "American history itself is full of extremes, of paradox, contradiction, and complexity." [1] In the field of religion in America, this is especially true. There are many times when individuals who claim to be Christian must ask: is this Christianity or is this culture? The issues of Kulturkampf (the struggle between the Church/religion and the State/culture in nineteenth century Germany) have, on a number of occasions, appeared in America in different clothing.

One area in which some aspect of the Americanization of Christianity has taken place is in the matter of theology. It is entirely fallacious to suggest that America produced neither a profound nor unique theology. Although the United States has espoused and followed rather faithfully the tenet of the separation of church and state, still it has been a nation which has understood its history, ideals, and destiny in religious terms. In considering again the theological beginnings of America, it must be remembered that: (1) no one group related to a single religious outlook originally settled in America. It is true that the Puritans tried for a theocracy, but it was not long until other groups appeared on the scene, and pluralism became the hallmark of American religion; (2) separation of church and state and religious liberty were not universally accepted. Some would even suggest that these arose as a matter of political expediency to unite otherwise diverse colonies; and (3) American thought was seldom, if ever, considered in the context of a united nation. Gradually, the country came to see that, in spite of differences, many concepts were commonly shared.[2] It is fair to suggest that precisely for these reasons of diversity, there was no alternative but to achieve a degree of unity in the country by accepting the separation of church and state and no laws respecting the establishment of an official religion.

Sydney Ahlstrom makes three general observations that would be worthwhile premises to consider before beginning the study of American theology. (1) Theological diversity exists throughout America. (2) The theology of America is more derivative than most European theology. (3) The theological influence shifted from England to Germany in approximately 1815.[3] He concludes by saying that we can be reasonably certain that "American churches will continue to champion their distinctive emphasis on lay-stewardship, democracy in government, individual freedom and voluntarism."[4]

The Americanization of Christianity is also to be noted in the study of the industrialization of America in the light of religion. Clearly, the Industrial Revolution arrived slightly later chronologically in America than in other parts of the Western World, but it did have and continues to have an in-depth effect upon the country. Religion and secular culture had allied themselves in the late nineteenth century in a way they had not done since the Bill of Rights. The church had usually exercised a prophetic voice of judgment on society in the early nineteenth century, but after the Civil War, churches had lost much of their prophetic power. Some have suggested that the acceptance of racial and industrial divisions in the late nineteenth century sapped the country's source of independent strength and effective outreach. The successful revival phenomena of the frontier could not be applied either easily or effectively to the urban industrial scene.

One of the leaders in America who tried to help the church meet the challenge of the urban centers and the industrial scene was Walter Rauschenbusch, a Baptist pastor. Rauschenbusch, of German extraction but raised in America, became concerned for the plight of the poor and deprived while serving as pastor in the "Hell's Kitchen" area of New York. It would appear that Rauschenbusch wanted to rally the middle class to a crusade that would "bring in the Kingdom of God." In a sense, Rauschenbusch had the social optimism of a man-produced Christian state. Reinhold Niebuhr, later in the twentieth century, provided a balanced corrective to Rauschenbusch's views. Niebuhr opposed identifying Christianity with the concept of social evolution. "Changing the social structure will not eradicate evil, since man is its source and he defies radical alteration." [5]

Most of the Protestant churches in America identified with the business community, because the bulk of their membership represented this social stratum. The Roman Catholic Church, which grew dramatically in the nineteenth century because of large numbers of immigrants, usually represented the working classes. Although there were a few religious reformers who sought to bridge the gap between worker and owner, the gulf often widened and became a religious division as well as a socio-economic one. It is inaccurate to assert that only theological liberals supported the social gospel concepts. The pioneer study of this subject was made by Timothy Smith in *Revivalism and Social Reform* through which he sought to show that evangelical Christianity was deeply concerned and anxious to improve social inequities before the Civil War. Although by the 1890's conservative Christianity had become wedded to Americal cultural values, there were efforts by many evangelicals to reach the whole man. [6]

The church, although denying rather emphatically the teachings of Darwin with reference to physical evolution, accepted some of his concepts relating to the social realm in the late nineteenth and early twentieth century. The church tended to preach the established American social and cultural values as the best. The Protestant ethic was reaffirmed, and its character was equated with success. The harder one worked, the better one would be, and hence the better one would fulfill the will of God. A hidden promise seemed to be that if one worked diligently, God would automatically reward him.

The statement, "God helps those who help themselves," received almost Biblical canonization and authority. In connection with such an ethic, one conceives even on the part of many evangelicals a tacit and subtle acceptance of salvation by works rather than by grace. The individualism of the early American, as well as that of the frontiersman, emerged again among Christians in twentieth century American churches. The layman had assumed a larger role in determining the basic emphasis of the churches. Paradoxical as it may seem, the liberty of the pulpit has not been challenged as long as the preacher does not "tread on toes," i.e. denounce free enterprise economics and success-oriented competitive individualism, or support expansion of the federal government or socialism. The suburban church sometimes becomes a "mutual admiration society," rather than a way station to rescue lost sinners. This phenomenon among the conservative churches and denominations tended to dull their evangelistic outreach, but even more the need for growth among those who had already been evangelized. In a sense in the twentieth century, classical Protestantism in America has adopted the "American Dream" as its own.

There are three other ways in which Christianity has been Americanized. Christian ideals have been gradually submerged to the culture. Oftentimes the Christian is not sure which things in his life come from Christianity and which, from his cultural pattern. It has been easier in America than elsewhere to articulate Christian ideals and virtues, yet practice something far different. When this situation has occurred at the higher echelons of society, it has brought discredit upon true Christianity. There is always a need for "real" Christianity, where Christian principles are believed, accepted, articulated, and supported. The American Christian of the twentieth century has frequently allowed his concern for material improvement and enjoyment of the better things in life to deaden, if not destroy, his Christian conscience and concern. The Christian frequently says, either verbally or unconsciously, "I believe in missions or the extension of the gospel, but I also believe in three full meals a day." To be asked to omit a meal for the cause of world hunger raises all sorts of issues. What good will it do, anyway? Why should the farmer be punished with the possibility of lower prices and loss of income? How easy it has become to forget the injunction of Jesus to give a cup of cold water in His name. To live for Christ with courage is a virtue for which we should strive. Christians of the twentieth century in America must constantly be in search of a Christian stand, for Christianity cannot be limited to a single country or become the civil religion of any society. The Americanization of Christianity in the twentieth century is taking place surely and certainly. We need not mourn that this is inevitably the case, but rather steer the ship of state through the deep waters of our Christian faith, making certain she docks at the significant ports guided by a certain rudder, the Lord Jesus Christ. Bishop James Armstrong of the United Methodist Church puts the issue of the Americanization of Christianity in true perspective and offers the means by which this Americanization of Christianity can bring victory. "A Christian patriot is one who, acknowledging fault and frailty, seeks to reflect the spirit and values of Jesus Christ above all else." [7] And finally, "Woe to those who are at ease in Zion, and to those who feel secure on the mountain" (Amos 6:1 RSV).

7.
Update on
Freedom

The hit movie of 1975 was "Jaws." This was the story of a shark whose menacing teeth violently devoured human flesh. In a recent political cartoon by Herblock, a takeoff was made from the movie "Jaws." [1] A shark with the words "undercover security operations" written on its underside swam fiercely, with exposed teeth, toward a female swimmer who had the words "individual rights" printed across her bathing suit.

A second political cartoon, which appeared ironically on Independence Day, July 4, 1975, bears mentioning. Indira Gandhi of India, who had just threatened the extinction of the world's largest democracy by the exertion of dictatorial powers, stood before a mirror with a club in her hand and asked, "Who's the Fairest One of All?" while a dead person with the words "civil liberties" labeled on his cloak lay at her feet.[2]

The points of these two political cartoons were explicit and serious. The one about a shark suggested that certain rights of Americans are in jeopardy. The accuracy of this suggestion will be illustrated by references to two types of recent infringements upon freedom. To begin with, freedom of the press, which is guaranteed in the First Amendment to the Constitution, has recently fallen victim to widespread suppression. As of June 27, 1975, six newsmen in four states were appealing jail sentences imposed on them for their unwillingness to reveal the confidential sources of their information. In several American cities reporters who had exposed official wrongdoing had been subjected to frameups, false arrests, intimidation, and surveillance. Judges in thirteen states had refused to allow news coverage of selected court trials. By court order a book about the Central

Intelligence Agency by Victor Marchetti and John Marks could be published only after 168 pages were purged. And the list could continue.[3]

There are those who charge that a free press is even suppressed in the publications of religious denominations. One influential editor of a denominational newspaper pointed to the importance of publishing bad news as well as good news in order not to deceive and manipulate readers. He then stated: "Our [Southern Baptist] denominational structure on the state level is not conducive to a free press. The growing and more prevailing organizational structure is to bring every denominational ministry under one umbrella and to put the control and direction in the hands of one committee and its staff."[4]

When this situation develops, claimed the editor, an official program exists which must be promoted and not questioned. The denominational newspaper for the state, he continued, then becomes the basic medium for promoting the program. Thus, only the good news is reported, and editorials lose their prophetic touch.[5]

Another example of infringement on freedom exists in the realm of technology and computers. In his 1974 book, *Attack on Privacy,* John Curtis Raines issued important warnings about the invasion of individual and group privacy by new technologies which convert private men and personal data into public records and by the law-and-order mentality which views opposition as subversive.[6] To demonstrate the need for his warnings, Raines pointed, for one thing, to credit cards which are capable of "tracking the patterns of our personal and associational activities, rendering us machine readable and retained."[7] Raines also called the reader's attention to computers and their potential for networking data systems containing diverse personal information on individuals' "bank records and credit ratings, educational and psychological testings, employment histories, political views, and protest activities."[8]

Raines then called for the legislative process to develop a legal concept of privacy which would be guided, among other things, by more attention to the citizen's right of access, avoidance of all unnecessary sharing of confidential information stored in computerized data banks, stricter attention to the dangers of compiling personal and group information, and a definition and encouragement of the view that " 'you have no right to ask that.' " [9]

An encouraging sign was the passage by Congress of the Privacy Act of 1974, which went into effect on September 27, 1975. In trying to interpret the law and its implications for Americans, one authority said that the Federal Government has gone to unwarranted lengths in collecting personal data, even beyond that which is really necessary, and has created the potential danger for misuse of the information gathered in dossiers. "The object of the law is to reduce the amount of information to be collected and to reduce the flow of information between agencies." [10]

As the political cartoon about a shark suggested that certain rights of Americans are in jeopardy, the cartoon about Indira Gandhi demonstrated that the whole concept of democracy and the civil and religious liberties which it affords can be quickly shattered. How ironic it was to read that Prime Minister Indira Gandhi, formerly an internationally-renowned sponsor of democratic ideals, had outlawed all the extremist political and religious parties in India as a further step in her surge to dictatorial power and her crackdown on opponents. This was simply an extension of her earlier emergency decree which suspended civil liberties in India. [11]

What do recent events in India have to do with freedom in the United States? If nothing else, the events can caution Americans to stay on guard in preserving their freedom. In commenting on the significance for Americans of the annual appearance of July 4, Jack Anderson stated in July, 1975, that the manner in which democracy shone brightly with a quality of hope and idealism in such a country as India and later fell into oblivion shows Americans how fragile is the seed of freedom planted in this country two centuries ago. [12] In another context the same columnist asserted that the preservation of freedom is directly proportionate to the initiative exerted to protect it. To be sure, "over the centuries, the rights of free men, though they be chiseled in stone, are not much stronger than the people's determination to defend them." [13]

The question still prevails: is it possible for the cherished ideals of democracy and freedom in this country to fall victim to forces of attrition, whether gradually or rapidly, as they obviously have in other countries? William V. Shannon recently claimed that: "the liberties that Americans enjoy can never be regarded as wholly secure. Despite our wealth, power and proud traditions, we are not immune to the appeal of a political demagogue or the risk of a military takeover implicit in having a large military establishment." [14]

Theodore H. White, who wrote the Pulitzer Prize-winning *The Making of the President—1960*, has prepared a new book entitled *Breach of Faith: The Fall of Richard Nixon*. In describing his purpose for writing the book, White zeroed in on the question just asked. After stating his belief that the government does stand for freedom and law, and after referring to the United States as one of the few countries where men and women can seek their future in freedom, White then said: "The Nixon people moved right up close on that; and, without knowing it, they squeezed on my freedom and yours. Maybe our individual freedoms can't be maintained. . . . But I believe that we should *try* to maintain our freedoms. And it's up to our government to keep it that way." [15]

What were some of the basic freedoms provided for in the foundational documents of this nation? Besides unalienable rights—including life, liberty, and the pursuit of happiness—provisions were also made for freedom of religion, speech, the press, assembly, and petition. These freedoms, along with others, were comprehensive in scope and integral to democracy. The forefathers of this country struggled to make these freedoms a reality, and they anticipated that the full achievement of these freedoms would make the United States a place where creativity, initiative, and imagination could reach unheralded heights.

In reflecting on the Bill of Rights, President Franklin D. Roosevelt stated in a nationwide radio address on December 15, 1941, that December 15, 1791, was a day which would always be important to liberty-loving men. On that day a new nation had formally adopted a declaration of human rights destined to influence the thinking of people in the United States and many other parts of the world.[16]

Freedoms in America have had to come to terms with threats, however. Private citizens have posited grievances against the federal government over alleged and unwarranted surveillance of their personal affairs by wiretapping and other means. Despite the Fourth Amendment to the Constitution, which says that "the right of the people to be secure in their persons, houses, papers, and effects, against unreasonable searches and seizures, shall not be violated . . . ,"[17] newspapers in recent years have carried stories in which apparently innocent families claimed that their homes were invaded and that they themselves were harassed by agents of the Federal Bureau of Investigation in search of narcotics.

Freedoms in contemporary American society also face other threats. Is it possible that the unalienable right called "life," which is mentioned in the preamble of the Declaration of Independence, should be understood only conditionally at a time when nuclear war, ecological kickbacks, population explosion, and energy depletion continually loom on the horizon as monstrous threats to the total definition of life in America? Of course, at each of these points, the moral question has to be inserted: to what extent is the deterioration of freedom in America a direct consequence of irresponsibility? The obvious answer to this last question, in far too many instances, is that irresponsibility is a sizeable factor.

Certain freedoms face financial threats. One of these is the right to an education or the freedom to learn. When the United Nations General Assembly adopted a Universal Declaration of Human Rights in 1948, one paragraph of the Declaration stated:

Everyone has the right to education. Education shall be free, at least in the elementary and fundamental stages. Elementary education shall be compulsory. Technical and professional education shall be made generally available and higher education shall be equally accessible to all on the basis of merit.[18]

Further, Elton Trueblood listed what he considered to be the six positive freedoms, that is, those freedoms which could be stated as moral imperatives and which are nearly universal in appeal. Alongside the freedoms to debate, to worship, to work, to live, and to serve, he stressed the freedom to learn.[19] Trueblood asserted that the financial responsibility for education should not be placed entirely on the individual or his family, since society at large gains from the educational achievements of its citizens. He pointed to the absurdity of limiting advanced learning to those financially wealthy, for the reason that the child in the poor family might be more trainable and educationally receptive than the child of a rich family. Trueblood then referred to the words of a university president who said that "we ought to be able to announce, honestly, that no person who is able to profit by a university education will ever be denied it because of his personal lack of funds." [20]

These pleas for the right to education and the freedom to learn are being confronted with a financial threat that is both contemporary and serious. One estimate claimed that the average cost for resident students in four-year private colleges will reach $4,391 in the academic year 1975-76, compared with $2,974 in 1970. Four-year public colleges will reach $2,679, compared with $1,783 only five years ago. These costs include tuition, fees, room and board, materials, transportation, and other vital expenses. Not just the poor suffer from these increased costs and accompanying inflation, for students from families in the middle-income range have particularly felt the brunt of these threats. The income of these families is often above the government's interpretation of need, and this disqualifies the students from federal assistance.[21]

Other freedoms, including the right to safety, face the constant threats of crime and violence. The crime rate in the United States is increasing more rapidly than the rate of economic inflation. FBI statistics show that the nation's crime rate was 18 percent higher for the first three months of 1975 than for the same period in 1974. How can Americans cultivate a sense of personal safety and the freedom of possession when robberies increased by 28 percent in a single year? [22]

In an era of women's liberation, female criminality is increasing in several categories between three and five times faster than male criminality. According to the United Nations crime prevention unit, robberies in the United States in the past five years have risen 300 percent among women, a much higher rise than among men. In the same period, homicides by women doubled or tripled those by males. These statistics point to a possible correlation between new opportunities given women and their involvement in crime.[23]

To demonstrate further the threat which crime poses for Americans, a recent Gallup Poll showed that a record 45 percent of Americans fear walking in their neighborhoods at night. In cities with over 500,000 residents, the figure reaches 56 percent. In addition, 19 percent admitted fears of household intruders.[24] A good reason for these fears, according to the poll, is that one fourth of all households in the United States were hit by crime at least once in the preceding twelve months, and this fraction shot up to one third among the households in cities of over 500,000 residents.[25] The fact that crime is the top concern of residents in cities of all sizes, even over economic concerns,[26] bears evidence of a threat to the personal safety of Americans which is achieving seemingly unstoppable proportions.

Still another freedom in American life has regularly faced a variety of threats. This freedom is religious liberty, including the separation of church and state, which is guaranteed by the First Amendment to the Constitution. As the constitutional basis for religious liberty, the American concept of the separation of church and state has frequently been called the most important contribution of America to world civilization.[27]

The separation of church and state suggests several important ideas. First, public officials cannot be required to take religious tests. Second, religious bodies cannot exercise authority over governmental matters. Third, government cannot exercise authority over religious matters. Fourth, government cannot endorse, establish, or give preferential treatment to any religious group or teaching, even if support or promotion is offered to all alike. Fifth, government funds cannot be used to support religious institutions. Sixth, support of any religious group or teaching cannot be forced upon anyone. Seventh, because religious faith is a voluntary matter within man and must not be subject to the coercions or restrictions of government, religious freedom shall be the possession of every person.[28]

Illustrative of the threats which have challenged the separation of church and state are those evidenced in the major issues confronted by the Baptist Joint Committee on Public Affairs, which had its origin under another name in 1936. Located in Washington, D.C., and sponsored by nine Baptist bodies in the United States and Canada, this agency is strongly committed to preserving the separation of church and state. Since 1936, four of the key issues with which it has dealt have been the public funding of nonpublic elementary and secondary schools, the federal funding of nonpublic higher education, the federal funding of sectarian hospitals, and religious exercises in the public schools.[29] On these and other issues the battles for and against separation of church and state have often been intense, and the Baptist Joint Committee has done a service to all Americans by working firmly against all forces hostile to this principle. Americans United for Separation of Church and State, a nonprofit educational corporation formed in the late 1940's and dedicated to preserving the constitutional principle of church-state separation, has also dealt with these and similar threats to this principle and has performed an equally admirable service.[30]

Perhaps the greatest threat to religious liberty has been the failure of American citizens to carry out the full opportunities afforded by this freedom. As one writer has stated:

> Religious liberty necessarily includes more than the right to believe and to worship. It must include the right to act and to witness freely in giving expression to one's religious views and convictions. Religious liberty is . . . basic to all other civil liberties, as is recognized in the American Constitution.[31]

Religious liberty will remain a vital part of American life only as long as initiative is exerted to maintain it by living out its ideals. In a similar vein, the religious historian Edwin Scott Gaustad wrote that freedom of religion in America allows religion to be as impotent as it wishes. "That freedom, however, can also be used to proclaim repentance, reform, and, if need be, even revolution. The struggle for "liberty and justice for all" is never wholly won, but only when that struggle ceases is the battle wholly lost." [32]

The final form of freedom to be discussed relates to religious bodies in America and centers on the right of individuals to interpret Scripture for themselves under the leadership of the Holy Spirit. Although taken from Baptist life, the points to be made are applicable to many denominational groups. Baptists have long been strong advocates of the freedom of conscience, and in line with the tradition of the Protestant Reformation, Baptists have extended this freedom into the arena of biblical interpretation by stressing the privilege of all men to interpret Scripture for themselves as guided by Christ. Any threat to an individual's privilege to interpret the Bible must be countered.

The Baptist heritage has been in line with Scripture and the practice of the early church in magnifying the priesthood of the believer and the related right of every church member to interpret the Scripture for himself. These two emphases both originated and perpetuate themselves in the freedom of conscience provided by God. This gift of liberty must be protected.

Immediately after Jesus died on the cross, "the curtain of the temple was torn in two, from top to bottom" (Matt. 27:51, RSV). The curtain was likely the one before the holy of holies, which was the innermost sanctuary of the Jerusalem Temple. Access to the holy of holies was confined to the Jewish high priest on the annual Day of Atonement when he atoned for the sins of Israel.

The generally followed interpretation of the tearing of the curtain "is that the holy of holies is now open to all men, not just to the high priest; for in Jesus Christ every man has direct access to the presence of God. . . ." [33]

This important biblical idea deteriorated during the Middle Ages, as lay believers were deprived of their priesthood and of their privilege to interpret Scripture. Fortunately, Martin Luther recovered the biblical stress on the priesthood of all believers and the competency of the individual to interpret for himself, and these two ideas became some of the distinctive convictions of the Protestant Reformation.

Since their beginnings in early seventeenth-century England, Baptists have viewed the priesthood of each believer as a cardinal principle of their faith. Little opposition has ever arisen to this doctrine. The complementary stress on the right and duty of individual Baptists to interpret Scripture for themselves has and does encounter occasional resistance. Religious groups need to counteract this threat by either affirming or reaffirming the legitimacy and necessity of individual interpretation.

To conclude, certain freedoms belong to persons because the latter are created by God. Other freedoms belong to persons because they live in the United States. Threats to both kinds of freedom are a permanent feature of history. Because of these threats, the freedom struggle is as old as man, beginning with Adam and Eve. The freedom struggle is as wide as man's personal, social, political, and religious experiences. The freedom struggle is inevitable and natural, as is the innate urge to express oneself creatively and with fulfillment.

Healthy forms of freedom deserve respect, and threats to them must be confronted. Obsession with "freedom for freedom's sake" cannot be tolerated, especially if it is not coupled with responsibility. The freedom struggle must be conditioned by biblical ethics. These ethics must impinge with authority on threats to freedom and on misuses of freedom. Americans, both as individuals and as a nation, both as seekers of freedom and as destroyers of freedom, would do well to hear the words of Ross Snyder who claimed that "healthy conscience is a necessity for freedom." [34]

8.
Using Freedom Responsibly

The previous chapter apart from the present one could place in the reader's mind a rather negative image of the freedom struggle in America. There are negative elements in this struggle, and to deny them would misconstrue reality. Threats to freedom and misuses of freedom do exist, and they deserve diligent confrontation.

Despite the problems related to the freedom struggle in America, there is a positive side to the story. Suggestions will be offered, which hopefully will generate both a wholesome understanding of freedom and constructive uses of freedom. These suggestions will be in the form of three general principles. The principles will be followed by several guidelines for dealing creatively with two aspects of the freedom struggle, namely, religious liberty and the right of individuals to interpret Scripture for themselves.

PRINCIPLES FOR UNDERSTANDING AND USING FREEDOM

Principle number one: persistent and sacrificial effort must be employed to gain and retain freedom.

One of the first lessons I remember learning from American history is the fact that freedom is never free. It always costs something in terms of struggle and agony and effort. It is never handed over to either an individual or a nation on a silver platter.[1]

With these words, John Claypool highlighted a cardinal truth.

Freedom is not an automatic and inevitable achievement for Americans. History records that "blood, sweat, and tears" have characterized the physical, religious, and ideological combats aimed at securing various types of liberty. Men and women have died in many wars both to acquire and preserve freedom for the United States. Colonial America witnessed the beatings of scores of people who believed that subjection to dehumanizing treatment was more preferable than conformity to a state church. James Madison beat off intellectual opposition and insisted on the values of incorporating the Bill of Rights into the national Constitution.

That the United States provides as many freedoms for its citizens as any country in the world is an affirmative note worth celebrating. Because of these freedoms and the deaths, beatings, and other sacrifices required to obtain them, modern Americans would do well to express gratitude and appreciation for the historical sufferings of their liberty-loving forefathers.

Initiative has been the key word. Americans have not attained a climate of freedom by assuming a posture of defense and silence. Aggressive action has been essential both to the procurement and maintenance of liberty. A word of caution for the future is in order. Present freedoms will not remain intact, and new freedoms will never come into existence without constant work. Regardless of the form of freedom at stake, it is imperative that Americans stay on guard. Citizens of tomorrow will live in slavery if citizens of today do not work as earnestly as their ancestors for freedom's sake.

Principle number two: freedom is legitimate only when exercised within the context of authority and certain limitations.

The desire for freedom can never become such an obsession that it abandons necessary restrictions. Otherwise, laws are broken, social customs are violated, and moral codes are set aside. Further, factionalism results when the desire for freedom overextends itself. Individuals, groups, and institutions, in this instance, "do their own thing," disharmony erupts, and relationships fracture as aimless freedom searchers cross paths and conflict.

Freedom can never be so free that it exists apart from authority. Typical constraints on freedom include the laws of the land, cultural patterns, institutional requirements, and biblical mandates, among others. Psychologically, physically, morally, spiritually, socially, and politically, it is essential that freedom operate within boundaries.

The Tennessee Supreme Court recently passed a ruling that fits into the subject of this discussion. The ruling made it illegal for the Holiness Church of God in Jesus Name, located near Newport, Tennessee, to continue the practice of snake-handling as part of its religious services.[2] The Court's belief was that its ruling did not violate the separation of church and state; rather, the ruling was designed to protect the physical safety of church members. The ruling of the five judges illustrated that even religious liberty must be practiced with certain conditions and restrictions placed upon it. In this instance of snakehandling, the authority of personal and social health had to take precedence over the continuing exertion of a dangerous form of freedom.

More positively, the second principle states that to become free is to assume responsibility for the rights of others, as well as for self, and not to infringe upon these rights. For the United States, this includes the rights of other nations. For American majorities, this includes the rights of minorities. For American corporations, this includes the rights of consumers. For American individuals, this includes the rights of other individuals. Freedom and responsibility for others must be mutually coexistent.

Principle number three: genuine freedom originates with God and makes sense only if related to the achievement of purpose in life.

In one Old Testament passage in which God addressed the Israelites, he identified himself as follows: "I am the Lord your God, who brought you forth out of the land of Egypt, that you should not be their slaves; and I have broken the bars of your yoke and made you walk erect" (Leviticus 26:13, RSV). The passage makes explicit that liberation for the Israelite nation evolved directly out of God's initiative. The concept of walking erect suggests that this new freedom created a conducive environment in which the Israelites could fulfil the intentions and purposes of God for them.

As the next chapter will show, American beginnings were saturated with biblical imagery, which conveyed that freedom for the new nation was God's gift and that God had a holy calling for the new nation. The former concept frequently became twisted both in the failure to acknowledge God as the source of liberty and in the temptation to insert human ingenuity in God's place. The latter concept often deteriorated into the belief that America's cause was always God's cause, and the result was misplaced priorities. The theme that freedom and justice are vital corollaries needs to ring with resounding impact through the coastlines, mountains, valleys, and plains of America. Neither is wholly attainable apart from God in whom all purpose exists.

GUIDELINES FOR UNDERSTANDING AND USING RELIGIOUS LIBERTY

One vitally important phase of the freedom struggle in America is the perpetual battle to maintain religious liberty. Although some Americans are more conscious of and interested in this issue than others, the nature of the struggle has ramifications for all Americans. Three guidelines will now be offered to help encourage a more adequate understanding and appreciation of the struggle, as well as more intense efforts to safeguard this foundational liberty in American life.

Guideline number one: realize that the United States is fortunate in possessing religious liberty, for this is not the case in many countries.

Citizens of the United States can begin to deal constructively with their failure to take full advantage of religious liberty by recognizing that such freedom is not a worldwide reality and that virtually millions of people are still struggling for this liberty. One specific example will illustrate the point.

Georgii Petrovich Vins is a Reform Baptist who is presently in a prison in Russia because of the absence of religious freedom in that country. (Reform Baptists are those who, like certain other religious bodies in Russia, believe that the best way to move forward under severe state pressure "is the direct approach of totally avoiding compromise and of using every opportunity to expose malpractices and put one's case openly to the oppressor first, and then to the whole world").[3]

For his religious activities, Vins was sentenced in November, 1966, to three years in a labor camp. After his release in 1969, his mother, who was a leader in the recently formed Council of Baptist Prisoners Relatives, was arrested at the age of sixty-five for sending information to the West and was sentenced to three years in a labor camp. Also, soon after Vins' release, he was appointed secretary of the Council of Churches of Evangelical Christians-Baptists, which included Reform Baptists, and became pastor of a church at Kiev. State pressure forced him to go into hiding in the summer of 1970 to fulfil his religious duties. A warrant was issued for his arrest in the same year, and he was finally captured on March 30, 1974. After being detained in poor health in the Kiev prison hospital, Vins was sentenced in January, 1975, to five years in a labor camp to be followed by five years' exile.[4]

In contrast, this kind of treatment cannot constitutionally be administered to a citizen of the United States for practicing his religious convictions. However, the struggle for religious liberty did not end with the ratification of the Bill of Rights in 1791. The struggle has continuing existence and makes itself known in many issues.

Guideline number two: realize that the battle to maintain the separation of church and state and religious freedom will be a permanent feature of American life and therefore deserves the constant support of all who favor it.

The First Amendment to the Constitution begins with the words, "Congress shall make no law respecting an establishment of religion, or prohibiting the free exercise thereof. . . ." James Leo Garrett is head of the J. M. Dawson Institute of Church and State at Baylor University and editor of the *Journal of Church and State*. Dr. Garrett recently took the two religion clauses in the First Amendment, namely, the "no . . . establishment" clause and the "free exercise" clause, and pointed to possible areas of struggle in the future.[5]

Concerning the "no . . . establishment" clause, one controversial issue with which the courts will likely have to deal relates to interpretations included in public school textbooks. Second, the constitutionality of appropriating public funds for church-related colleges and universities will continue to be an important issue. Third, the question of taxation of church-owned property will demand solution. Fourth, church-state issues may arise as they relate to the military chaplaincy. Other church-state issues impinging on the "no . . . establishment" clause will also require discussion.

Respecting the "free exercise" clause, cases involving Black Muslims will likely increase, although it is difficult to tell at this point whether new Hindu and Buddhist-derived movements in this country will encounter problems with the political order. Sunday closing laws may continue to be challenged by Jews and other Sabbatarians and possibly by Friday-worshiping Muslims, who may view the laws as a violation of "free exercise." Also, the Supreme Court will likely have to deal again with conscientious objection to combatant military service. Other issues difficult to foresee, but relating to "free exercise," will no doubt appear before the year 2000.

Since these and other church-state issues are likely to come to the forefront in the immediate future, the courts of America will have the enormous responsibility of continuing to clarify and defend the constitutional principle of church-state separation. As the foundational concept behind religious liberty, church-state separation is essential to the health of America.

All citizens who support this concept must verbalize their beliefs, write letters to editors and Congressmen, and stay informed. Subscriptions to *Church & State* (published by Americans United for Separation of Church and State), to the *Journal of Church and State* (published by Baylor University), and to *Report from the Capital* (published by the Baptist Joint Committee on Public Affairs) will enable one to stay up-to-date in church-state matters.

Guideline number three: fulfil the demands and opportunities of religious liberty.

The purposeful intent behind the First Amendment achieves fruition only when Americans take full advantage of the freedoms which it offers. The freedoms of speech, press, peaceful assembly, and petition are maintained only by being activated. Similarly, "the 'free exercise' of religion can only be truly meaningful where there is genuine, vital, and meaningful exercise thereof." [6] To be sure, "the future significance of the 'free exercise' of religion depends on the vigor and vitality of the religious communities more than on the verdicts of the judiciary in our pluralistic society." [7]

Religious liberty cannot be approached simply from a defensive perspective. No one, of course, can deny the necessity of resisting all forms of encroachments on this vital precept of American life. In these instances, defensive measures of many kinds are perfectly in order. The key point is that the preservation of church-state separation and religious liberty hinges much more directly on offensive strategies. Whether Protestant, Catholic, Jew, or otherwise, this means living out one's faith in committedness. The occasional nod to God must be replaced by affirmative action in favor of the things relating to God. Intelligent understanding and practice of one's faith must supersede a passive spiritual life-style.

GUIDELINES FOR UNDERSTANDING AND USING INDIVIDUAL FREEDOMS

Another important phase of the freedom struggle relates to

religious bodies in America and the right of individual members to interpret the Bible for themselves. As pointed out in the last chapter, this spiritual freedom can sometimes be violated by subtle creedalistic tendencies. The following five guidelines are practical ways by which individuals can protect their right to interpret the Bible and meet resistance to this form of spiritual liberty with a prayerful firmness. Although applicable to many religious denominations, the suggestions are based on observations of Baptist life—that which is most familiar to the writers.

Guideline number one: acknowledge that disagreement over doctrinal issues always has been and continues to be a legitimate feature of Baptist life.

To illustrate, a few of the issues which have been tossed to and fro in Baptist thinking have been limited atonement versus general atonement, open communion versus close communion, and the acceptance of alien immersion versus the rejection of alien immersion. Baptists have differed over the appropriateness of congregational singing, foot washing, and deaconesses.

The fact that Baptists have taken various positions on these and other issues has not meant that those on one side of an issue were true Baptists and those on the other were not. All were Baptists. The beauty of the priesthood of all believers is that it provides flexibility for interpretation. To deprive a church member of his right to differ on an issue is to deprive him of his priesthood. Still, there are certain key beliefs to which persons must adhere in order to be Baptists. Examples are the baptism only of believers in Christ, a church membership, regenerated by the Holy Spirit, and the Bible as the inspired word of God.

Guideline number two: recognize that Baptists are non-creedal.

Rather than create precisely-formulated creeds to every element of which a rigid commitment has been expected, Baptists have developed confessions of faith. Written by the hundreds, these confessions simply have been guidelines for interpretation, rather than authoritative and binding documents.

Baptist confessions have varied in content throughout the centuries. That Baptists historically have frequently modified and altered their doctrinal statements is clear evidence that the priesthood of all believers has been taken seriously. The members of contemporary Baptist churches possess the equal privilege and duty of regularly taking a hard look at their doctrinal convictions without fear of reprisal on the part of those who may disagree.

Guideline number three: realize that the individuality, background, and prejudices of each Baptist are different.

The biblical approach is to accept the value of persons, even though these persons may differ radically from one another. The distinctiveness of individual Baptists will inevitably generate variance in thought and expression about biblical and doctrinal ideas. This dynamic interaction is helpful for the individuals, the churches, and the denomination.

A ten-year-old Baptist may be completely justified in describing a Baptist belief in a way that is totally unlike the description of a fifty-year-old Ph.D. who teaches philosophy and theology. A Baptist who spent most of his life as a Roman Catholic may differ in interpretation with a Baptist who has known nothing but Baptist life. Even a person's sex can cause him or her to take a particular stance about doctrine. Thank God for the priesthood of believers which insists on a healthy respect for persons!

Guideline number four: remember that every person is created in God's image.

Among other things, to be created in this manner means that God expects man to be creative. A crucial kind of creativity is theological reflection. All persons are compelled to explore the vital dimensions of our faith. The examination of one's origin, reason for being, the basis for one's doctrinal stances, and the future are merely a few of the timeless considerations of mankind.

Baptists would be remiss in discouraging their peers from engaging in the freedom of creative spiritual thought, even if the results of such reflection vary. A proper appreciation for the worth of fellow Baptists and the value of their ideas is an integral feature of the priesthood of all believers. All are created in God's image, but God does not expect that all will be alike. Unlikenesses sometimes register themselves in legitimate differences in interpretation.

Guideline number five: work graciously but firmly against the efforts of dominant personalities who try to force their interpretations on others.

A passive acceptance of the doctrinal pronouncements of a person who appears overly aggressive and far too definitive is a disservice on two counts. A person does disservice to himself by being so dependent on the thinking of another that he never engages his intellectual and spiritual capacities in the area of Baptist beliefs. Second, the person who pretends to have the ultimate answer to every question does disservice to himself in assuming a characteristic reserved for God alone.

One can learn much from fellow Baptists in Sunday School and Church Training groups, in worship services, and in other church meetings. A person must not confine what he knows about the Bible and Baptist doctrine to what certain dominant personalities can give him. He must learn the fine art of thinking for himself and seeking the presence and guidance of Jesus Christ. A multitude of new insights are available from a responsible encounter with the Bible, the Holy Spirit, and the Baptist heritage.

The full advantages of responsibly used freedom are yet to be comprehended and employed by most Americans. Still, the good news is that freedom awaits, with open arms, morally healthy exploration and utilization. The future is an unlimited receptacle for the wholesome values that can emerge from a stimulating encounter among persons, God, and liberty.

9.
The American Dream: Intact or Exploded?

An attempt to define the American dream can be an elusive discipline. *One reason is that not all Americans have the same dream.* Some early immigrants came to this country in search of religious freedom. Others came to seize vast economic opportunities. Still others came with a sense of adventure and the desire to explore. A multiplicity of goals and purposes continues to characterize the American people.

A second reason is that there seems to be such a wide disparity between the original intent of certain parts of the dream and the subsequent working out of the dream in concrete actions. Thus, the question has to be raised: is the real American dream that idealism which preceded and governed the formation of the nation, or is it the realism by which the country actually functions? The implication of the question is that the corporate dream of the United States is not static but changing.

A third reason is that the American dream is such a nebulous phenomenon that it is subject to widely-varying interpretations. The highly skilled political scientist who was reared in an affluent family may delineate the dream quite differently from another person who has had fewer advantages. The peculiar circumstances of one's life will obviously condition one's appraisal of the dream, regardless of the common denominators in standard interpretations. The present writers hope simply to help clarify the dream from the perspectives with which they view it.

How can a person arrive at the general traits of the American dream? One approach is to examine selected national and religious documents and hymns, which manifest certain themes and ideals which have long penetrated American thought and can be considered at least part of the dream. The Declaration of Independence indicates that the truths are self-evident "that all men are created equal; that they are endowed by their Creator with certain unalienable rights; that among these, are life, liberty, and the pursuit of happiness." The pledge of allegiance claims that the United States is "one nation, under God, indivisible, with liberty and justice for all." The second stanza of "The Star-Spangled Banner" asserts: "And this be our motto: 'In God is our trust!' " and similarly the coins in our pockets state, "In God we trust." "America, the Beautiful" describes this country as filled with "spacious skies," "amber waves of grain," "purple mountain majesties," and "fruited plain."

Assuming that these ideals are part of the American dream, a series of dilemmas confront the nation. If it is so obvious that "all men are created equal; [and] that they are endowed by their Creator with certain unalienable rights," why was it that the average annual income of Indian families in the United States was less than $2,000 in 1972,[1] and why was President Kennedy able to state as a moral issue in 1963 that the Negro baby born in America in that year had about "one-half as much chance of completing high school as a white baby . . .; one-third as much chance of completing college; one-third as much chance of becoming a professional man; twice as much chance of becoming unemployed; [and] about one-seventh as much chance of earning $10,000 a year . . ."?[2]

Further, if it is so clear that this country is "one nation, under God," in a sense of commitment to the divine way, why was it that in 1972 there was one divorce for every 2.7 marriages in America, and why is it that one child in every six is forced to live in a one-parent family before he is eighteen?[3] And why was it that about 800,000 cases of gonorrhea were reported in the United States in 1973?[4]

If it is so evident that "In God we trust," why is it that according to a recent study 38 percent (or 30,000) of the enlisted men in the United States Navy confessed that they are boozers with drinking problems that they described as "critical," "very serious," or at least "serious"? [5]

If America is the land of "spacious skies," how can one account for massive levels of air pollution in many urban areas, and why are research groups asserting that the fluorocarbon gases used as propellants in aerosols are eating away the ozone layer of the earth's atmosphere and thus exposing people to dangerous radiation from the sun and increased skin cancer? If America is the land of "amber waves of grain" and "fruited plain," what explanation does one have for the daily hunger of thousands of citizens, and why do weekly food purchases represent a disproportionate percentage of the income of multitudes of people? If America is the land of "purple mountain majesties," what response must be made to the destruction of mountains by reckless strip mining?

What has been written to this point only opens the door in an effort to define the American dream and shows how certain features of this dream are crumbling before the very eyes of Americans. It is necessary to plumb the depths of definition a little more carefully and to look at both the positive and negative sides of the American dream. Especially important is the need to see how the concept of success is tied up in this dream. Two recent books which deal with this subject, in remarkable detail and which present cogent arguments, are especially helpful. The more important is the book by Robert Benne and Philip Hefner entitled *Defining America: A Christian Critique of the American Dream.* [6] The second, by Robert N. Bellah, is entitled *The Broken Covenant: American Civil Religion in Time of Trial.* [7]

The place to begin is with America's understanding of her origin, for this understanding has exerted a heavy influence on subsequent thought and action. Several key concepts entered the American dream quite early. One was the idea of the "American Adam." The person arriving on the American shores was viewed as innocent. Theologically, he had a second chance. Previous sins were wiped away simply by his presence in a new land, and a new beginning was in the making. The "American

Adam" had enormous potential and was characteristically optimistic. Things were going to get better and better.

In one sense, the idea of the American Adam was theologically beneficial. The Adam of the Old Testament had a unique and special relationship to God. Through the image of the American Adam, immigrants to the new land believed themselves to be in a particularly close relationship with God. On the other hand, this biblical motif as applied to Americans was theologically naive. Its optimistic view of man as innocent and of life as getting better and better neglected the tendency toward evil which had saturated the total history of man.

Complementary to the motif of the American Adam was the image of America as the "New Israel," or the "Promised Land." Driven deeply into the American consciousness by the Puritans, this image persisted in the theme that Americans were a "chosen people" who had a "manifest destiny." Ezra Stiles, president of Yale University, described the new nation in 1783 as "God's American Israel" [8] and asked, "May we not see that we are the object which the Holy Ghost had in view four thousand years ago when he inspired the venerable patriarch with the visions respecting his posterity?" [9] Stiles' comments reflected a rather common form of American messianism.

According to Stiles, not only was America God's true Israel, but she had heroes who paralleled those of ancient Israel. Describing the American army raised to engage in the struggle for independence, Stiles wrote that

Congress put at the head of this spirited army the only man on whom the eyes of all Israel were placed. . . . This American Joshua was raised up by God . . . for the great work of . . . conducting this people through the severe, the arduous conflict, to liberty and independence. . . . [10]

Although the term "manifest destiny" was apparently not used until the 1840's, [11] the feeling behind it existed much earlier. In its simplest terms "manifest destiny" suggests that God and

America are partners and that God has in some sense chosen America to be his instrument. The identification of America as the chosen race has been a key factor in America's foreign and domestic policy throughout her history.

Although the biblical concept of chosenness implies a call to mission and service, this concept as applied to America frequently disintegrated into a confusion of national purpose and God's will. Rather than seek diligently after the intentions of God for America, America often set her own goals, implemented her own plans, and finally called on God to applaud her ideals and successes. The inevitable result of this logic was civil religion.

Related to the idea of chosenness was what might be called "republican millennialism." Since the kingdom of God was virtually equated with the republican political system launched by the new nation, it followed naturally that the millennium had begun. Timothy Dwight, later to succeed Ezra Stiles as president of Yale University, wrote in 1776 that the progress of liberty, science, and empire had advanced from east to west since the beginning of time. Further, each succeeding empire had been more glorious than the one before it. Dwight then added that the empire of North America would be both the last on earth and the most glorious of all. In this empire the perfection of temporal things would be accomplished, and human greatness would reach its supreme height.[12]

Not only was America viewed as a paradise, but she was also viewed as a wilderness filled with savage Indians, high mountains, and other obstacles. The wilderness theme was not a totally negative concept, however, for when related to the wilderness experience of Jesus subsequent to his baptism, the wilderness experiences of early Americans were seen as times for purification.

The previously mentioned elements in the self-image or dream of Americans had their rootage in the Judeo-Christian tradition as expressed in such terms as the "American Adam," "New Israel," "Promised Land," "chosen people," "millennialism," "paradise," and "wilderness." One additional biblical term which fitted early into the American dream was "covenant." The Puritans placed much stress on a proper covenantal relationship between man and God and between man and man. Covenantal togetherness helped balance out the Puritan emphasis on individual conversion.

A secular understanding of the myth of America's origin has also evolved. "It exhorts us to shake free of the limiting past in a struggling ascent toward the realization of promise in a gracious future." [13] It was through the actualizing of this understanding of the myth of origin that the American concept of success developed. First, on the road to success Americans have attempted "to shake free of the limiting past." This has often resulted in playing free and easy with the past and with leaving mass wreckage on each successive frontier. The victimized have included Indians, blacks, used consumer products, blighted land, inner-city areas, and others. Thus, in grasping for success, Americans have frequently sought individual gain by shaking free of covenantal relationships with nature, God, and men, especially those people in minority groups.

Second, in a fight for success, Americans have been caught up "in a struggling ascent." Initiative, creativity, and personal sacrifice have been maximized. Benne and Hefner stated that the inner-directed self-starter was the only man who could make the struggling ascent. This helped place a strong voluntarist motif into the American culture. "Americans are the 'can do' people. . . . The strong sense of taking responsibility for one's own destiny with as little dependence on outside help as possible has been and is a valued part of the American character." [14]

Self-independence and pragmatism became basic ingredients in the American individual's understanding of himself. The capacity for self-sustenance arose in some measure out of necessity, as when frontiersmen faced the gracious but capricious nature of various wildernesses. The transferral of this capacity into dimensions of life, in which covenantal relationships might have been more appropriate, often left frustrated Americans in a state of frenzied loneliness. The elevation of the "can do" pattern of individual and national isolationism into the failure to acknowledge the God who saturated the early American dream resulted in the ultimate form of self and national deprivation.

Thus, competition is an important part of the American way. Competition permeates the American educational system, the national love for sports, and the country's concern to be number one among the nations of the world in as many areas as possible. The idea is both that the best will win, and that the best will be obtained from each competitor. Two problems which tend to arise in this phase of the American dream are: (1) what to do with those who either cannot or will not compete, and (2) the disrespect for authority and covenant within those who compete with no sense of dependence on others. To put it in another way, those who view competition as a syndrome to avoid, either because of handicap or an uneasy feeling about the values of perpetual contests for superiority, and those who compete outside the boundaries of human concern and justice, find themselves in a minority. As such they have to face the apprehensions of a restless majority, for whom competition is the key to life.

Third, the American dream sees success as heading "toward the realization of promise in a gracious future." The dream has presumed that there are no social, geographical, economic, or political restrictions on man. Opportunities are unlimited, goals are achievable, and little can stop Americans from advancing. This aspect of the dream has had to come to terms with closing doors. Social, geographical, and economic expansion are not nearly so unlimited as they once seemed. Further, the "gracious future" which once favored success may not be so favorable to progress as it thrusts itself into history with a population explosion, unending inflation, and an energy crunch, among other things.

Contemporary and historical evidence demonstrates that the American dream has its dark side. The American Adam is not as innocent as once believed. To be sure, there is sometimes a nightmarish quality in the role of America as the New Israel.

Americans have abandoned covenants, elevated self, destroyed many people and a good deal of nature, found themselves not so powerful as they once thought, and see the future coming at them with a not-so-gracious thrust. Optimism is being displaced by realism.

Perceptive persons from the beginning of American history have reminded Americans of the flaws of original sin, and of the ongoing evil attached to their dream, but the decade of the 1960's "has decisively revealed the ambiguity of the American myth and reality. Events of nationwide significance constantly bombarded the American consciousness in that period." [15] These events included the surfacing of the racial problem in the civil rights movement and the Black Power movement; the rise of the Indian movement for self-determination; the growth of massive ecological concern and related concern for overpopulation; poor nutrition, and overall health care; an intensification of efforts to deal with abuses of the consumer; the reaching of the zenith of the peace movement and the war in Indochina; the appearance of increased student dissent; the heightened prevalence of urban decay and transition; the emergence of the women's liberation movement; a rise in concern for the elderly; attainment of a new high point in the drug problem; and increased inflation. [16]

The American dream is in many respects a magnificent dream. It calls for equality of opportunity, certain unalienable rights for all citizens, trust in God, liberty and justice for all, and other positive features. These kinds of elements, if actualized, would be worthy of Scripture and God. They are not, however, and American life moves along at a much less spiritual rate. Inconsistences and ambiguities plague the American dream and displace the spiritual possibilities of the dream with a life-style that could lead to eventual defeat. Is the American dream intact or exploded? The negative parts of the dream appear to be more intact than the positive. The Christian hope has the potential of reconstructing the positive features, aiding in the demise of the negative features, and achieving consonance between the ideals of the dream and the practical expression of the dream, both in the life of the nation and the individuals comprising it. The next chapter will relate the Christian hope to the American dream.

10.
The Christian Hope and the American Dream

As has been suggested, the past several years have manifested conditions which demand that Americans take a hard look at their dream and concept of success. It is time to ask some penetrating questions about this recent unveiling of truth.

Is America willing to acknowledge that her problems and sins are sometimes more real than she pretends and that she is not so innocent as once presumed? Is America willing to examine the causes and dynamics of her evil and try to perceive what this evil says about the nation? As questions of dependence emerge in the face of ambiguity, is America willing to take seriously the affirmations about trusting in God which permeate key national documents and appear on billions of pieces of coins and currency? Is America willing to retrieve her past to see whether she has lived up to her possibilities and acted responsibly in her covenantal agreements with nature and citizens, especially those persons in minority groups? Is America willing to accept her finitude and the inevitability of restrictions on her heretofore unstoppable uses of freedom? Is America willing to face up to the fact that her success story has often involved "a compulsive concentration on the means of attaining success with little concern about the broader terms in which it is to be measured"? [1]

These questions obviously require religious responses. An evaluation of the American dream will first involve an effort to delineate the meaning of authentic Christian hope. Second, it will be necessary to redefine success in the light of this hope and to look at various phases of the American dream for the purpose of reaffirming certain elements and suggesting modifications of other parts of the dream. The basic guide for arriving at the Christian hope will be the Bible.

To begin with, Christian hope is an inclusive kind of hope. History, man, and creation are all wrapped up in the Christian understanding of hope. Hope as fulfilled in the context of God's purpose is not a segregated hope, but an integrated hope. The entire cosmos will cohere in unity in God's presence when hope attains future consummation. Some foundational biblical passages behind the inclusiveness of the Christian hope are these:

> In the beginning God created the heavens and the earth. Then God said, "Let us make man in our image, after our likeness. . . ." And God saw everything that he had made, and behold, it was very good (Gen. 1:1,26a,31a, RSV).[2]

These verses make clear that God is the author of history, of creation, and of man. The Christian hope both originates and culminates with God.

The inclusiveness of the Christian hope has clear evidence in biblical passages which describe God's redemptive purposes for the total scope of his creation. The individual person is included in God's redemptive concern. Paul stated that "if any one is in Christ, he is a new creature; the old has passed away, behold, the new has come" (2 Cor. 5:17). The redemptive plan is broader than the individual man, however, for "God was in Christ reconciling the world to himself" (2 Cor. 5:19), and "the creation itself will be set free from its bondage to decay and obtain the glorious liberty of the children of God" (Rom. 8:21).

The redemptive and inclusive elements of the Christian hope find full expression in Matthew 25. In a parable of judgment, Jesus referred to the coming of the Son of man who would separate all the nations of the earth, as a shepherd separates sheep from goats. The Son of man, according to Jesus, would then invite the righteous to inherit the kingdom provided for them:

> . . . for I was hungry and you gave me food, I was thirsty and you gave me drink, I was a stranger and you welcomed

me, I was naked and you clothed me, I was sick and you visited me, I was in prison and you came to me (Matt. 25:35-36).

The hope of the righteous resided both in the way that they related comprehensively to the needs of hurting humanity and in the quality of therapy applied to these needs. The Christian hope, therefore, urges that America evaluate her dream for the specific purpose of determining whether her national priorities are designed primarily to meet the needs of her citizens. If a country exists simply to meet the needs of its government, big business, the military, or any other single segment of national life, apart from an all-embracing concern for the total population, then the hope of the country is inadequate.

Besides being inclusive and redemptive, the Christian hope is characterized by justice. There is no discrimination, manipulation, or depersonalization. To the contrary, says 2 Peter, "according to his [God's] promise we wait for new heavens and a new earth in which righteousness dwells" (3:13). The justice and judgments of God will extend beyond an individual application and will impinge with authority upon nations:

Just and true are thy ways,
O King of the ages!
Who shall not fear and glorify thy name, O Lord?
For thou alone art holy.
All nations shall come and worship thee,
for thy judgments have been revealed (Rev. 15:3-4).

Amos was the Old Testament prophet of justice *par excellence.* After revealing the transgressions of Damascus, Gaza, Tyre, Edom, Ammon, Moab, and Judah, and the respective punishments that would result, Amos focused on the transgressions of Israel. He was particularly incensed at the oppression of the poor by the rich. Amos claimed that the Israelites had "turned justice into poison and the fruit of righteousness into wormwood"

(Amos 6:12). With forcefulness of expression, Amos admonished Israel to "hate evil, and love good, and establish justice in the gate" (Amos 5:15). The Christian hope is that justice will prevail in America.

While this chapter was being written, two news items relating to the national budget appeared in successive issues of a local newspaper. The first indicated that the House of Representatives had passed an $111.89 billion defense appropriation bill, which would then be sent to the Senate, and that this represented a cut in the budget request of the President by more than $9 billion. The total budget item included about "$40 billion for personnel, $35 billion for operations, $25 billion for military hardware procurement, and $12 billion for research and development." [3] The same newspaper reported on the next day that the President had vetoed a $2.75 billion child nutrition bill, and that this threatened the termination of a school breakfast program which daily feeds 1.8 million low-income pupils.[4]

Although Congress overrode the veto of the child nutrition bill a few days later,[5] the question still must be asked: are justice and equity predominant features of a budgetary breakdown proposed by the executive branch of the United States when the military gets about $112 billion while hundreds of thousands of poor school children get no breakfast? This is just one example of many misplaced priorities in America. The Christian hope is that such misplacements will be rectified. Fortunately, Congress provided the rectification needed with the child nutrition bill. The words of the Lord as revealed through Amos need a new hearing: ". . . Let justice roll down like waters and righteousness like an everflowing stream" (Amos 5:24).

Further, the ultimate hope is God himself and therefore is a present hope, as well as a future hope. Jeremiah referred to God as the "hope of Israel, its savior in time of trouble" (14:8), and the apostle Paul spoke of Christ as the "hope of glory" (Col. 1:27). To be sure, hope is such a present reality that Proverbs 13:12 asserts: "Hope deferred makes the heart sick, but a desire fulfilled is a tree of life." Hope in God has a direct relationship to the purification of one's present life. John believed that "every one who thus hopes in him [God] purifies himself as he is pure" (1 John 3:3). Despite its importance, present hope must be conditioned by the realization that Christian hope reaches its climax only in the future. As Paul wrote, "If in this life we who are in Christ have only hope, we are of all men most to be pitied" (1 Cor. 15:19).

From the Christian perspective, genuine hope does reside in God. The uninformed could be deceived into thinking that all America genuinely believes this after reading about Congressional prayer breakfasts, worship services in the White House, the placing of hands upon Bibles in courtroom settings, the engraving of religious phrases on coins, and the inserting of "under God" in the pledge of allegiance to the American flag. Many of these references to God and things of religion are superficial and deify a national dream in behalf of civil religion.[6]

The processes of American government include regular mention of the word "God." Ideally, this mention would involve at least a partial understanding of the nature of God and his purposes for this country. One has to wonder whether this comprehension exists, however, in the face of oppression for minority groups, humiliation for the poor on welfare programs, tax breaks for the undeserving, and huge profits for the unprincipled, while the "have not's" are defeated even further. "And the American taxpayer, without any voice in the matter, is forced to worship at the shrine of the gods of war and provide military arms for all sides of virtually every conflict around the world."[7]

In view of this description of Christian hope, a redefinition of success is now in order. Traditionally, success as a vital part of the American dream, as was dealt with in the previous chapter, has involved three key elements: (1) a shaking free of limits imposed by the past, (2) engagement in a struggling ascent characterized by personal initiative and sacrifice, a keen sense of competition, and a strong exertion of self, and (3) an optimistic thrust into a gracious future that is filled with unlimited opportunity and few, if any, restrictions.

Unfortunately, this concept of success in America has all too often resulted in a denial of historical and covenantal relationships with God, man, and nature. A lot of wreckage has been created as Americans have attempted to rid themselves of past limits. Also, the voluntaristic and competitive motifs have played havoc with those who were unable or unwilling to compete and who became disdainful of authority. Further, in its rush toward a gracious future, the American view of success has sometimes lived superficially with the pretense that it has no boundaries.

The Christian hope demands several modifications in the American dream and the view of success that is wrapped up in it. First, history and the covenantal relationships that have developed in it must be treated with more dignity. America must treat history with the full awareness that it was launched by God. America must treat persons with the cognizance that each of them was created in God's image. America must treat nature and all its resources with more of a caretaking, rather than destructive, attitude. Tied in with all this must be the firm acknowledgment that America has certain limits (constitutional, moral, and others) which she would do better to stress than to dismiss. Success requires that America relate to all parts of God's creation (past and present) with redemptive goals in mind.

The construction and preservation of covenantal relationships are vital to the health of American life. Early immigrants to America developed covenants in civic, as well as ecclesiastical, life. As early as 1620, the Pilgrims on the ship *Mayflower* entered an agreement known as the Mayflower Compact. The signers of this mutual pledge bound themselves to contribute to the general good of the Plymouth community and to give obedience to the laws of the colony.[8] Also, the early inhabitants of Providence Plantations in Rhode Island of the late 1630's were required to assent to a covenant similar to the Mayflower Compact.[9] The values of such covenants were that they increased the respect of colonists for one another, of colonists for government, and of government for colonists.

Is it possible for the American dream to become so totally

fragmentary and diversified that even the commom denominators of the dream will begin to vanish? With the government going one way, civic institutions going another, and individuals going a third, covenantal agreements can deplete themselves. A renewal of relationships among citizens—between government and citizens—with nature, and with God can replace irresponsible and rugged individualism and self-dependence with substantive pledges of mutuality and concern.

Second, a major alteration of the American view of success must come at the point of insisting that Americans not be so individualistic and competitive in their climb up the ladders of life that they bypass their responsibilities to those unable and unwilling to compete. To both must be supplied the principle of the Good Samaritan. The Christian hope includes justice and love for all.

Those unable to compete include children, the aged, the poor, the sick, and the handicapped, among others. Those unwilling to compete include the non-motivated, the person who finds deep meaning in life apart from a highly competitive environment, and many more. For those who cannot help themselves, America can extend a helping hand—not through tokenism and arrogance, but through programs and relationships which magnify the self-image of the helpless and assure them that they are viewed as first-rate citizens. For those who refuse to compete in all the standard ways, America can assume an empathetic stance. To the non-motivated, she can provide new thrusts in education. To the person whose meaning in life does not consist in competition, she can ask if lessons are to be learned from them. All Americans deserve justice in the truest and biblical sense.

Third, the success element in the American dream must be conditioned by a healthy respect for authority. Self cannot be elevated so that there is no dependence on fellow citizens or on God. God is the hope of America. It is not possible to circumvent his presence. To deny the need for God and fellow citizens is spiritual and civic suicide.

For an individual to presume that he can operate outside all boundaries and limits results in mental depletion, psychological deception, immoral libertinism, physical exhaustion, and borders on usurpation of divine rights. This problem becomes significantly compounded when it finds expression on the national level. Just as individual Americans live within frameworks that must be honored, so does America.

When the success syndrome results in imperialistic actions, manipulative exertions, depersonalizing tendencies, immoral impingements, constitutional abandonments, and a violation of simple covenantal agreements with God, man, and nature, then it is time for serious introspective reflection to take place. The liberty and freedom treasured so highly in America achieve fruition not by over-extension into the rights of other individuals, organizations, cities, states, and countries, but by a proper respect for the rights of these entities through the cultivation of affirmative and constructive relationships.

Fourth, the optimistic element in the American approach to success should not be blind. It should be a realistic optimism. There are numerous limits on the future of America, and she must realize this. Land can run out, natural resources can be depleted, inflation can become overbearing, and the list can go on indefinitely. The Christian ethic demands a new sense of responsibility to opportunities, the environment, and all citizens. A wide open future is possible only through hope in God. He alone provides life everlasting. Faith in God, not a blind and optimistic attachment to self-attainment, is the kind of hope America needs.

America, the Christian hope beckons you to deny yourself and render more meaningful service to citizens and to the world alike. America, the Christian hope implores you to confess your sins, make amends with the victimized, and live with economic, political, social, and religious integrity. America, the Christian hope appeals for you to reaffirm covenantal commitments to man and nature and to meet the moral expectations of God.

Notes

INTRODUCTION

1. C. Welton Gaddy, "Significant Influences of Baptists on Politics in America," *Baptist History and Heritage,* XI: 5-6, January, 1976.

2. *Ibid.,* p. 7.

3. Harold W. Brown, "Baptist Churches as Moral Courts," *The Chronicle,* V:89, April, 1942.

4. W. Morgan Patterson, "Discipline in Baptist Churches and Culture on the Early Frontier," *Review and Expositor,* LXI:539, Winter, 1964.

5. William Warren Sweet, *Religion in the Development of American Culture, 1765-1840* (New York: Charles Scribner's Sons, 1952), pp. 145-46.

6. Constant H. Jacquet, Jr. (ed.), *Yearbook of American and Canadian Churches, 1974* (Nashville: Abingdon Press, 1974), pp. 119f.

7. A. H. Newman (ed.), *A Century of Baptist Achievement* (Philadelphia: American Baptist Publication Society, 1901), p. 339.

8. R. Orin Cornett, "Education, Southern Baptist," *Encyclopedia of Southern Baptists,* 1958, I, 389.

9. *U.S. News & World Report,* LXXIX:39-41, October 13, 1975.

10. *Ibid.,* p. 39.

11. Duke K. McCall, "Public Psychiatry on National TV," *The Tie,* 44:15, October, 1975.

12. *Ibid.*

13. Penrose St. Amant, class lecture, Southern Baptist Theological Seminary, 1972.

14. William A. Norgren (ed.), *Forum: Religious Faith Speaks to American Issues* (New York: Friendship Press, 1975), p. 5.

15. T. B. Maston, "Criticism and Commitment," *Western Recorder,* 41:3, 14, October 19, 1961. Maston applied these four options to the Baptist denomination alone.

16. Penrose St. Amant, class lectures, Southern Baptist Theological Seminary, 1972.

CHAPTER 1

1. Elbert Thomas, *This Nation Under God* (New York: Harper and Brothers, 1950), p. 44.

2. See P. Colquhoun, *A Treatise on Indigence,* London, 1806, as quoted in R. R. Palmer, *The Age of Democratic Revolution* (Princeton: Princeton University Press, 1959), p. 191.

3. *Ibid.,* p. 192.

4. *Ibid.,* p. 190.

5. John Adams Works (1851), IV, 292-293 quoted in Palmer, Op. cit., p. 192.

6. See David Ramsey, *History of the American Revolution* (Philadelphia: R. Aitken and Son, 1789).

7. Palmer, pp. 193-194.

8. Benjamin Franklin, *Articles of Belief and Acts of Religion,* as quoted in Norman Cousins, *In God We Trust* (New York: Harper Brothers, 1958), p. 16.

9. Norman Cousins, *In God We Trust* (New York: Harper Brothers, 1958), pp. 16-17.

10. *Ibid.,* p. 17.

11. *Ibid.,* p. 18.

12. *Ibid.,* p. 20.

13. *Ibid.,* p. 50.

14. *Ibid.,* p. 51.

15. *Ibid.,* p. 62.

16. *Ibid.,* p. 117.

17. *Ibid.,* p. 301.

18. Douglas Adair and Marvin Harvey, "Was Alexander Hamilton a Christian Statesman?" *Alexander Hamilton,* ed. Jacob E. Cooke (New York: Hill and Wang, American Century Series, 1967), pp. 239 ff.

19. *Ibid.,* p. 240.

CHAPTER 2

1. George Bancroft, "The Office of the People in Art, Government and Religion" (An Oration Delivered before the Adelphi Society of Williamstown College in August, 1835), in *Literary and Historical Miscellanies* (New York, 1855).

2. Norman Cousins *In God We Trust* (New York: Harper & Brothers, 1958), p. 42.

3. E. S. Gaustad, *Dissent on American Religion* (Chicago: University of Chicago Press, 1973), p. 43

4. James Bryce, *The American Commonwealth* (New York, 1889) I, 306.

5. Quoted by Gerald N. Grob and Robert N. Beck in *American Ideas* (London: Free Press of Glencoe, 1963), I, 227.

6. See Carl L. Becker, *The Declaration of Independence, A Study in the History of Political Ideas* (New York: Alfred A. Knopf, 1942) for a detailed study of the Declaration of Independence.

7. John Alden, *A History of the American Revolution* (New York: Alfred A. Knopf, 1969), p. 242.

8. Stanley Cohen and Lorman Ratner, eds., *The Development of an American Culture* (Englewood Cliff: Prentice Hall, Inc., 1970), p. 6.

9. Julian P. Boyd, *Papers of Thomas Jefferson* (Princeton: Princeton University Press, 1950), I, 494-5.

10. The Constitution of the United States and Amendments, Amendment Article I as quoted in *Documents of American History,* ed. Henry Steele Commager (New York: Appleton-

Century-Crofts, 1968), I, 146.

11. A helpful discussion of these concepts can be found in the article by Wilbur G. Katz, "Religion and Law in America," James W. Smith and A. Leland Jamison, *Religious Perspectives in American Culture* (Princeton: Princeton University Press, 1961), pp. 53-68; and James E. Wood, Jr., "Religious Liberty and Public Affairs in Historical Perspective," *Baptist History and Heritage,* IX: 154-67, July, 1974.

12. Winthrop S. Hudson, *American Protestantism* (Chicago: University of Chicago Press, 1961), p. 67.

13. James Wood, "Religious Liberty and Public Affairs in Historical Perspective," *Baptist History and Heritage,* IX: 160, July, 1974.

CHAPTER 3

1. Edwin S. Gaustad, *A Religious History of America* (New York: Harper and Row, 1966), p. 6.

2. *Ibid.,* p. 7.

3. W. W. Sweet, *The Story of Religion in America* (New York: Harper and Brothers, 1950), p. 2.

4. Winthrop S. Hudson, *American Protestantism* (Chicago: University of Chicago Press, 1951), p. 3.

5. James W. Smith and A. Leland Jamison, *The Shaping of American Religion* (Princeton: Princeton University Press, 1961), p. 24.

6. Perry Miller, *The New England Mind: The Seventeenth Century* (New York: Macmillan, 1939), pp. 464-484.

7. Alice Felt Tyler, *Freedom's Ferment* (New York: Harper and Row Publishers, 1962), p. 5.

8. Gaustad, p. 50.

9. Perry Miller, "The Contribution of the Protestant Churches to Religious Liberty in Colonial America," *Church History,* IV: 57-66, March, 1935.

10. Cedric B. Cowing, *The Great Awakening and the American*

Revolution: Colonial Thought in the 18th Century (Chicago: Rand McNally and Co., 1971), p. 11.

11. Sweet, p. 171.

12. Sydney E. Mead, *The Lively Experiment* (New York: Harper and Row Publishers, 1963), p. 37.

CHAPTER 4

1. Winfred Garrison, "Characteristics of American Organized Religion," *Annals of the American Academy of Political and Social Science,* CCLVI: 17, March, 1948.

2. Thomas Jefferson, "Address to Danbury Baptist Association," January 1, 1802, as quoted in Joseph Martin Dawson, *America's Day in Church, State and Society* (New York: Macmillan Company, 1953), p. 25.

3. James W. Smith and A. Leland Jamison, eds., *Religious Perspectives in American Culture* (Princeton: Princeton University Press, 1961), pp. 163-164.

4. Sydney Mead, *The Lively Experiment* (New York: Harper & Row, 1963), p. 52.

5. Cedric B. Cowing, *The Great Awakening and the American Revolution: Colonial Thought in the 18th Century* (Chicago: Rand McNally and Co., 1971), p. 223.

6. William G. McLoughlin, *Isaac Backus and the American Pietistic Tradition* (Boston: Little, Brown and Company, 1967), p. 231.

7. Cowing, p. 224.

8. John Callender, *An Historical Discourse on Civil and Religious Affairs of the Colony of Rhode Island,* Third ed. (Boston: Thomas H. Webb and Company, 1843), p. 70.

9. See James E. Wood, Jr., "Religious Liberty and Public Affairs in Historical Perspective" *Baptist History and Heritage,* IX:154f., July, 1974, for a thoughtful, carefully documented historical summary of religious liberty as an integral part of Baptist history. Other studies in this vein are C. Emmanuel

Carlson, "Religious Liberty and American Culture," *Review and Expositor* (Winter, 1964), pp. 506f., and James E. Wood, Jr., "Baptists and Religious Liberty," *Southwestern Journal of Theology,* (April, 1964), pp. 38f.

10. Wood, *Baptist History and Heritage,* p. 167.

11. David Benedict, *A General History of the Baptist Denomination in America and Other Parts of the World* (New York: Sheldon, Blakeman and Co., 1856), p. 421.

12. W. W. Sweet, *Religion on the American Frontier: The Baptists* (New York: Henry Holt and Co., 1931), p. 3.

13. See C. C. Goen, *Revivalism and Separatism in New England, 1740-1800* (New Haven: Yale University Press, 1962), for a detailed discussion of the progression of the Separates to Separate Baptists during the Great Awakening and Revolutionary Period.

14. See Robert Semple, *A History of the Rise and Progress of the Baptists in Virginia* (Richmond: John O'Lynch, 1810) provides details of the Baptist struggle in Virginia by one who was an active primary observer. Leland's involvement is discussed in detail in L. F. Greene (ed.) *The Writings of the Late Elder John Leland Including Some Events in His Life* (New York: G. W. Wood, 1845).

15. See John B. Boles, *The Great Revival: 1787-1805* (Lexington: University of Kentucky Press, 1972). Boles attempts to "reconstruct the multifaceted religious mind of southern evangelicals," p. xi.

16. Albert H. Newman, *A History of the Baptist Churches in the United States,* Revised edition (Philadelphia: American Baptist Publication Society, 1898), p. 336.

17. W. W. Sweet, *Revivalism in America* (New York: Charles Scribner's Sons, 1944), p. 117.

18. See W. W. Sweet, "The Churches as Moral Courts of the Frontier," *Church History* (March, 1933), pp. 3f., for a discussion of this concept.

19. James W. Smith and A. Leland Jamison, eds., *Religious Perspectives in American Culture* (Princeton: Princeton University

Press, 1961), p. 18. The article by Will Herberg offers a helpful survey of the influence and role of religion in American education. That the article was prepared before the Supreme Court decision of 1962, which prohibited official prayer in public schools, tends to make the article somewhat dated. A helpful study on the development of denominational colleges may also be found in W. W. Sweet, *Religion in the Development of American Culture 1765-1840* (New York: Charles Scribner's Sons, 1952), pp. 162-183. For additional discussion related to Baptists see Charles W. Deweese, "Education and the Baptist Experience in America," *Search* (Winter, 1976).

20. John Lee Eighmy, *Churches in Cultural Captivity* (Knoxville: The University of Tennessee Press, 1972), p. x.

21. *Ibid.,* p. vii.

22. Smith and Jamison, p. 5.

23. *Ibid.*

24. See Martin E. Marty, *The Pro and Con Book of Religious America: A Bicentennial Argument* (Waco: Word Books, 1975), p. 73. This unique book offers some helpful thoughts on this subject in the two chapters devoted to this matter. "A Promised Land for All Races," pp. 67-76 and "A Racist Nation," pp. 71-80.

25. Alexis de Tocqueville, *Democracy in America* (New York: Alfred A. Knopf, 1945), p. 32.

26. Arthur B. Rutledge, *Mission to America* (Nashville: Broadman Press, 1969), p. 235.

27. *Annual,* Southern Baptist Convention, 1940, p. 263.

CHAPTER 5

1. As quoted by Martin Marty, "Churches Behaving Civilly," *Fides et Historia,* VII: 4, No. 2, Spring, 1975.

2. George Grant, *Lament for a Nation* (Toronto: McClelland and Stewart Limited, 1970), pp. 2-3.

3. As quoted in William W. Sweet, *Religion in the Develop-*

ment of American Culture (New York: Charles Scribner's Sons, 1952), p. vii.

4. James W. Smith and A. Leland Jamison, *The Shaping of American Religion* (Princeton: Princeton University Press, 1961), p. 162.

5. *Ibid.,* p. 163.

6. H. Richard Niebuhr, *The Social Sources of Denominationalism* (New York: Henry Holt and Company, 1929), p. 19.

7. Edwin S. Gaustad, *A Religious History of America* (New York: Harper and Row, 1966), p. 132.

8. A helpful summary of each of these groups may be found in Alice Felt Tyler, *Freedom's Ferment* (New York: Harper and Row, 1962).

9. Sweet, p. 282.

10. Whitney R. Cross, *The Burned Over District: The Social and Intellectual History of Enthusiastic Religion in Western New York, 1800-1850* (Ithaca, New York: Cornell University Press, 1950), p. 144.

11. Sweet, p. 286.

12. Niebuhr, p. 105.

CHAPTER 6

1. Martin E. Marty, *The Pro and Con Book of Religious America: A Bicentennial Argument* (Waco: Word Books, 1975), p. 11.

2. Frederick Sontag and John K. Roth, *The American Religious Experience: The Roots, Trends and Future of American Theology* (New York: Harper and Row, 1972), pp. 12-13.

3. James W. Smith and A. Leland Jamison, *The Shaping of American Religion* (Princeton: Princeton University Press, 1961), pp. 234-235.

4. *Ibid.,* p. 321.

5. Sontag and Roth, p. 144.

6. See George Marsden, "The Gospel of Wealth, the Social

Gospel, and the Salvation of Souls in Nineteenth Century America," *Fides et Historia,* V: 10-21, Spring, 1973.

7. James Armstrong, *The Nation Yet to Be:* Christian Mission and the New Patriotism (New York: Friendship Press, 1975), p. 120.

CHAPTER 7

1. "Jaws," *The Tennessean,* June 25, 1975, p. 13.

2. "Who's the Fairest One of All?" *The Tennessean,* July 4, 1975, p. 17.

3. Jack Anderson, "News Suppression Epidemic Has Hit U.S.," *The Tennessean,* June 27, 1975, p. 15.

4. C. R. Daley, Jr., "Publish and Conceal Not," *Western Recorder,* August 16, 1975, p. 4.

5. *Ibid.*

6. John Curtis Raines, *Attack on Privacy* (Valley Forge: Judson Press, 1974), pp. 12-13.

7. *Ibid.,* p. 12.

8. *Ibid.*

9. *Ibid.,* p. 120.

10. "Government Snooping—How to Fight Back," *U.S. News & World Report,* LXXIX:21, September 22, 1975.

11. Edward Cody, "Indira Outlaws 26 Extremist Parties in India," *The Tennessean,* July 5, 1975, p. 1.

12. Jack Anderson, "The Marvel of the Ages: This Fourth of July, 1975," *The Tennessean,* July 4, 1975, p. 17.

13. Anderson, "News Suppression," p. 15.

14. William V. Shannon, "Can Democracy Last If Morality Withers?" *The Tennessean,* September 18, 1975, p. 14.

15. "Behind the Lines," *Reader's Digest,* 106:16, May, 1975.

16. Frederick C. Packard, Jr. (ed.), *Great Americans Speak* (New York: Charles Scribner's Sons, 1948), p. 90.

17. *Ibid.,* p. 123.

18. Stanley I. Stuber, *Human Rights and Fundamental Freedoms in Your Community* (New York: Association Press, 1968), p. 127.

19. Elton Trueblood, *Declaration of Freedom* (New York: Harper and Brothers, 1955), pp. 54-70.

20. *Ibid.,* p. 55.

21. Martha V. Gottron, "Middle Income Students: College Cost Crunch," *The Tennessean,* May 16, 1975, p. 14.

22. "1st Quarter Crime Rate Up by 18%," *The Tennessean,* July 22, 1975, p. 1.

23. Gene Kramer, "Female Crimes Outstrip Male," *The Tennessean,* May 15, 1975, p. 91.

24. "Nearly Half of America Considers Nation Unsafe," *The Tennessean,* July 29, 1975, p. 9.

25. "Crime Hits One House in Four," *The Tennessean,* July 31, 1975, p. 13.

26. "Nearly Half," p. 9.

27. James E. Wood, Jr., "Religious Liberty and the Separation of Church and State," *Baptist History and Heritage,* 9:160, July, 1974.

28. J. Terry Young, "Your Heritage: Religious Freedom," *Western Recorder,* July 19, 1975, p. 3.

29. Stan L. Hastey, "Major Issues in Baptist Public Affairs, 1936-1971," *Baptist History and Heritage,* 9:194-207, October, 1974.

30. "Landmarks of Religious Liberty," *Church & State,* 28:7-8, September, 1975.

31. Wood, p. 166.

32. John Eagleson and Philip Scharper (eds.), *The Patriot's Bible* (Maryknoll, N.Y.: Orbis Books, 1975), p. 55.

33. Frank Stagg, "Commentary on Matthew," *The Broadman Bible Commentary,* vol. 8 (Nashville: Broadman Press, 1969), p. 247.

34. Ross Snyder, *On Becoming Human* (Nashville: Abingdon Press, 1967), p. 61.

CHAPTER 8

1. John R. Claypool, "The Struggle for Freedom," *The Baptist Student,* XLIX:7, May, 1970.

2. Kenneth Jost, "Court's Decision Out of Step with Its Own Views," *The Tennessean,* September 14, 1975, p. B-2.

3. Michael Bourdeaux, "Baptists in the Soviet Union Today," *Baptist History and Heritage,* X:230, October, 1975.

4. Roger Hayden, "Church and State: English and Russian Baptist Perspectives," *Baptist History and Heritage,* X:165, July, 1975.

5. James Leo Garrett, "The Two Religion Clauses of the First Amendment: Retrospect and Prospect," in *Our Heritage of Religious Freedom* (Silver Spring, Maryland: Americans United for Separation of Church and State, 1975), pp. 42-43.

6. *Ibid.,* p. 43.

7. *Ibid.,* p. 44.

CHAPTER 9

1. John Eagleson and Philip Scharper (eds.), *The Patriot's Bible* (Maryknoll, N.Y.: Orbis Books, 1975), p. 10.

2. *Ibid.,* p. 6.

3. "Family Enrichment: Mission of the Board's Family Ministry Section," *Facts and Trends,* 19:1, June, 1975.

4. "Venereal Disease," *The Tennessean,* May 15, 1975, p. 37.

5. Jack Anderson, "The U.S. Navy Has Its Problems in Drinking," *The Tennessean,* May 19, 1975, p. 13.

6. Philadelphia: Fortress Press, 1974.

7. New York: Seabury Press, 1975.

8. Winthrop S. Hudson (ed.), *Nationalism and Religion in America: Concepts of American Identity and Mission.* (New York: Harper and Row, 1970), p. 64.

9. *Ibid.,* p. 65.

10. *Ibid.,* p. 68.

11. Julius W. Pratt, "The Origin of Manifest Destiny," *The American Historical Review,* XXXII:798, July, 1927.

12. Hudson, pp. 60-61.

13. Benne and Hefner, p. 8.

14. *Ibid.,* p. 11.

15. *Ibid.,* pp. 41-42.

16. *Ibid.,* p. 43.

CHAPTER 10

1. Robert N. Bellah, *The Broken Covenant: American Civil Religion in Time of Trial* (New York: Seabury Press, 1975), p. 148.

2. All succeeding biblical passages also come from the Revised Standard Version.

3. Edmond LeBreston, "House Passes $111.89 Billion Defense Bill," *The Tennessean,* October 3, 1975, p. 12.

4. "Ford Pens Veto to Breakfast in Schools Aid," *The Tennessean,* October 4, 1975, p. 1.

5. "School Lunch Veto Beaten by Congress," *The Tennessean,* October 8, 1975, p. 1.

6. James Armstrong, "How Thick the Wall? (The Role of the Church in the Political Arena)," in *Our Heritage of Religious Freedom* (Silver Spring, Maryland: Americans United for Separation of Church and State, 1975), p. 3.

7. *Ibid.,* p. 4.

8. Williston Walker, *The Creeds and Platforms of Congregationalism* (New York: Charles Scribner's Sons, 1893), p. 89.

9. James D. Knowles, *Memoir of Roger Williams, the Founder of the State of Rhode Island* (Boston: Lincoln, Edwards and Co., 1834), p. 120.